# FREDERICK DOUGLASS

# FREDERICK DOUGLASS

## SELF-MADE MAN

### TIMOTHY SANDEFUR

CATO INSTITUTE

WASHINGTON, D.C.

Paperback ISBN 978-1-944424-85-5
eISBN 978-1-944424-86-2

Library of Congress Cataloging-in-Publication Data available.

Jacket design: Jon Meyers.
Jacket image courtesy of Hillsdale College.
Printed in Canada
www.cato.org

Also by Timothy Sandefur

*The Permission Society*

*Cornerstone of Liberty: Property Rights in 21st-Century America*
(coauthored with Christina Sandefur)

*The Conscience of the Constitution*

*The Right to Earn a Living: Economic Freedom and the Law*

# Dedication

*To the memory of Evan Scharf and John Norton.*
*"You may well cherish the memory of such men."*
*—Frederick Douglass*

# Contents

# Author's Note

In February 1818, Frederick Douglass was born to an enslaved mother on a Maryland plantation. By the time he died, at the age of 77, he was a world-renowned intellectual, bestselling author, sought-after speaker, international diplomat, bank president, and civil rights leader. As the nation pauses to commemorate the bicentennial of this remarkable man's birth, it is worthwhile to recall not just his own triumphant narrative, but the ideas and principles that he articulated better than almost anyone in American history.

A curious feature of existing books about Douglass is that they often focus more on his heroic personal story than on the ideas that formed the basis of all his work. In one sense, that's understandable: few American biographies are as inspiring as his. But Douglass was also a scholar and writer of immense skill and a political leader whose actions were consistently guided by his commitment to the principles articulated in the Declaration of Independence: all people are born free and equal, with inherent rights, which nobody may justly violate. Each person owns himself (or herself; Douglass was an outspoken feminist), and nobody is entitled to dictate our choices.

Some Douglass scholars disregard critical aspects of his political views. They emphasize his belief in armed resistance to slavery but downplay his belief that the Constitution was fundamentally an anti-slavery document, or that black Americans must integrate into white society, rather than separate themselves from it. For example, in 2009, Angela Davis—a former member of the Black Panthers and the Communist Party, and a recipient of the

Soviet Union's Lenin Peace Prize—published an edition of *Narrative of the Life of Frederick Douglass*; in it, she focuses on the injustice and illegitimacy of slavery but makes no mention of Douglass's later embrace of the Constitution and rejection of the anarchist version of abolitionism that he espoused at the time he wrote the *Narrative*. Her notes make no mention of Douglass's hostility to communism, his skepticism of labor unions, his unequivocal opposition to black nationalism, or his allegiance to limited government and free enterprise. Other scholars have openly condemned Douglass for his "bourgeois" belief in "laissez-faire,"[1] and his "blinkered" "faith in the miraculous workings of the free labor market,"[2] and have even claimed he was "being manipulated" by the ideology of "self-possessive individualism."[3]

In fact, individualism was the centerpiece of his creed—a creed he embraced proudly and with full consciousness. The theme of his life was well stated in the title of his most popular composition, the lecture "Self-Made Men," which he delivered over 50 times in the last half of his life. "Personal independence is a virtue," he declared in that lecture, "but there can be no independence without a large share of self-dependence, and this virtue cannot be bestowed. It must be developed from within."[4] Douglass—who taught himself to read, then taught himself the principles of political philosophy, and then rose through his own efforts to become one of the nation's foremost intellectuals—was preeminently a self-made man. And in his mind, the United States should be a society for the self-made.

Independence, pride, and personal and economic freedom were to his eyes the natural consequences of the basic principle of equality that lay at the heart of the American dream—a dream all people, without regard to race, deserved a chance to pursue. Douglass believed, and with good reason, that if Americans would adhere to their Constitution, theirs would be a free, dynamic, sometimes rough and boisterous society, but one in which people could and should *make* themselves. And he had little patience for fashionable nostrums—such as socialism and spiritualism—that offered fantasies of revolutionary transformation or utopia, or promised to relieve people of the burden of *making* themselves. When today's scholars downplay or criticize his belief in individualism, private property, free enterprise, and constitutionalism, it says more about them than about him.

Two centuries after his birth, it is worth taking a fresh look at Douglass's life—both as a spokesman for and a representative of this creed of individualism and freedom. In some ways a conservative, in other ways a revolutionary, he both espoused and lived the central idea of his work: we own ourselves and must be free to make ourselves the best people we can be.

This book would not have been possible without the kind help of many people. Thanks most especially to Deborah J. LaFetra, John McKee Barr, Christina Sandefur, Roger Pilon, Jonathan Blanks, and Craig Biddle.

# Introduction

Like most people born into slavery, Frederick Douglass never knew his exact birthdate. He once made an educated guess, picking February 14, 1817, but late in life, he learned that he had been off by a year. Still, to hear him tell it—and it is always best to hear him tell it, in the three versions of the autobiography he published—he was in a larger sense born in August 1834. That was when, pushed to the end of his endurance, he wrapped his hands around the throat of Edward Covey and held on until blood ran down his fingers.

The 16-year-old Douglass had been sent to Covey to be broken when his master, Thomas Auld, decided Douglass was too insolent. Covey ran a sort of corrective labor camp for slaves with too much spirit. For a year, he brutally ground away at Douglass's sense of self-worth, putting him to hard labor from sunrise to sunset, giving him only small servings of tasteless food, and subjecting him to random punishments for minor infractions. For the first six months, Douglass was whipped once a week, with sticks or rawhide thongs.

Such treatment was an essential component of the system of racial chattel slavery that dominated the culture and economy of the early United States, particularly in the South. But while the master class treated slaves as beasts of burden, they still knew in their hearts that each person in servitude nevertheless remained a *person*, and that this ineradicable humanity was the weak point in the whole system of slavery. It was the basic source of all the uprisings, rebellions, conspiracies, running away, and troublemaking on the plantations where millions of enslaved black people labored every day. Demolishing their humanity was therefore the masters' primary mission. Arbitrary punishment meted out for the breaking of subjective, undefined rules—for "impudence" or "disrespect"[5]—was just part of the master's systematic assault on the slave's sense of individualism. Bondsmen were meant to know only terror, suspicion, and dependence, lest they form alliances and rise up against the masters. They were to be kept illiterate and uneducated, and their natural affections—including among families—were to be broken or manipulated to serve the master's interests. Their lives were to be subjected to no rule other than the master's will. Thus, Covey would beat Douglass arbitrarily, or sneak up on him while he was working and lash out at him for failing to accomplish some impossible task—all with the goal of reducing him to the status of a paranoid and obedient animal.

Eventually, it worked. After weeks of relentless abuse, the young man felt his spirit break, and "[t]he dark night of slavery closed in upon me."[6] After one especially savage attack, he tried his last option, walking miles in the hot summer sun to his owner's store to beg for mercy. Thomas Auld only shrugged and sent him back.

Somehow, on the return to Covey's farm, Douglass found something new within himself. The next morning, when the slave-breaker appeared out of nowhere and attacked again, he resisted. "Whence came the daring spirit necessary to grapple with a man who, eight-and-forty hours before, could with his slightest word, have made me tremble like a leaf in a storm, I do not know," he wrote. "[A]t any rate, I *was resolved to fight.*"[7] He flipped Covey to the ground and began fending off his blows. The standoff lasted for hours. At last the attacker stumbled away, pretending he had won. But Douglass knew the truth. And Covey never beat him again.

That confrontation came to epitomize Frederick Douglass's long life. Recounting the tale, as he often did, he would quote a line from Lord Byron: *Who would be free, themselves must strike the blow.* Freedom was not, and could never be, a gift given to black Americans by the white majority. If it were regarded that way, freedom would then exist only at white society's will, to be revoked whenever whites chose. Douglass rejected that notion. He believed that only by taking responsibility for their own fates—through hard work, education, and diligence; by undertaking the duties of citizenship on the battlefield, in elections, and in the jury box; by demanding and meriting an equal place in democratic society—could black Americans achieve and deserve their own liberty. This, he believed, was entirely within reach if the United States would rise up and live out the true meaning of its basic creed: that all people everywhere are entitled to freedom—freedom to become what they can be. There was no end to what free people could accomplish—and there was no reason the black man could not achieve what other races had, in politics, law, literature, industry, or warfare: "If you will only untie his hands," Douglass affirmed, "I think he will live."[8]

# 1. Early Years: 1818–1826

Frederick Douglass was born in 1818 on the Wye House planta-tion, which is still standing near Easton, Maryland. His mother gave him the name Frederick Augustus Washington Bailey.* Wye House's owner, U.S. Sen. Edward Lloyd, was often away in Washington; during those times, his property—including the more than 1,000 humans he owned—was administered by Captain Aaron Anthony, who also owned his own small farm and a few slaves, including Douglass.

Anthony was also likely Douglass's father, although Douglass never knew for sure. As for his mother, he had only flickering mem-ories of nighttime visits, and a vague notion that she resembled the drawing of an Egyptian pharaoh he later found in a book. "The prac-tice of separating mothers from their children," he explained, "was a marked feature of the cruelty and barbarity of the slave system; but it was in harmony with the grand aim of that system, which always and everywhere sought to reduce man to a level with the brute."[1]

In his mother's absence, young Frederick was raised by his Grandmother Betsey, who lived in her own log cabin, apart from the slave quarters on Anthony's Holme Hill Farm, in what is now the tiny community of Cordova. Douglass described his early childhood as joyful, though obviously poor. He could spend his days fishing in the mill pond and chasing squirrels. But at about seven years old, he was taken to live at the "Great House," 17 miles away on the main Lloyd property.

---

*Douglass also went by the name of Johnson, and possibly by other names, at various times. Here we will call him by the name he made famous.

There he was placed in the care of Aunt Katy, a cruel woman who resented being forced to tend to Frederick, partly because it took away from the resources she could bestow on her own children.[2] She often denied him food, either so she could feed the others or as punishment. One evening, when the hunger became unbearable, he stole a handful of corn; he had set it on the hearth to warm when his mother appeared on one of her rare visits. He quickly scarfed up the kernels, but not before his mother realized what was happening. Taking pity on him, she gave him a gingercake and, while he gobbled it down, "read Aunt Katy a lecture which was never forgotten."[3] But the victory was short lived. It proved to be the last time he saw his mother, and he remained in the custody of the merciless Aunt Katy.

Too young for field work, Frederick was assigned small errands, cleaning tasks, and the meager education that was allotted to slaves. This consisted mostly of discipline and rudimentary religious instruction. Increasingly, in the decades that followed, the Christian churches of the United States would struggle over the morality of slavery, but on the plantation, the message was unambiguous: slavery was a holy institution, decreed by God, who made some to rule and others to serve. This propaganda was a powerful device for weakening the incipient individualism of those kept in servitude, strengthening the resolve of the tiny master class, and assuaging guilt among whites who, like Captain Anthony, owned few slaves, or none at all. Mark Twain, a rough contemporary, recalled of his own Missouri boyhood that he "had no aversion to slavery" growing up. "I was not aware that there was anything wrong about it. No one arraigned it in my hearing; the local papers said nothing against it; the local pulpit taught us that God approved it, that it was a holy thing, and that the doubter need only look in the Bible if he wished to settle his mind . . . ; if the slaves themselves had an aversion to slavery they were wise and said nothing."[4]

Alongside religious sanction, the master class used other techniques to keep the racial categories in line and prevent the uprisings that were always their nightmare scenario. This was one of the key distinctions between American slavery and the versions practiced in other nations and other times. Among the Greeks and Romans, for instance, slavery was based not on ideology, but on class status and the fortunes of war. During the first half of the 19th century, American slave owners developed the color line into a comprehensive philosophy that tightened slavery's vise. Anti-miscegenation laws, laws forbidding the teaching of slaves to read, and laws that restricted free black Americans from traveling or becoming citizens became more common. But it was not just upper-class whites who drew and enforced the color line. Poor whites were just as likely to embrace racism as was the master class. As William Freehling observes, "contradictory cultures love scapegoats."[5] Douglass was to find as a laborer, and even as an abolitionist, that racism was just as common among working-class whites in the North, to whom it served economic and even psychological needs, as it was among southerners. After the Civil War, when race-hatred impeded the efforts of industrial leaders, white workers still clung to it, demanding that their labor unions admit only white members and that managers refuse to hire blacks or Asians.

The legal, ideological, racial, and religious rationalizations for slavery were intended primarily to reinforce the mores of that institution among whites. Far more practical and ruthless measures of punishment and indoctrination maintained the institution among the slaves. The overriding point of this training— one might say, domestication—of a young slave was to obliterate individuality. The institution's survival depended on that. It was the theme of everything slave masters inflicted on the oppressed race—from illiteracy to the disruption of the family to the arbitrariness of punishments to the satirical names masters often gave their slaves—Zeus or Jupiter, for instance. "The first work of slavery is to mar and deface those characteristics of its victims which distinguish men from things," Douglass explained. Thus, the master's "first business" was to "blunt, deaden, and destroy the central principle of human responsibility" and specifically the slave's *conscience*:

> Conscience is, to the individual soul, and to society, what the law of gravitation is to the universe. It holds society together; it is the basis of all trust and confidence; it is the pillar of all moral rectitude. Without it, suspicion would take the place of trust; vice would be more than a match for virtue; men would prey upon each other, like the wild beasts of the desert; and earth would become a *hell*.

> Nor is slavery more adverse to the conscience than it is to the mind. This is shown by the fact, that in every state of the American Union, where slavery exists, except the state of Kentucky, there are laws *absolutely* prohibitory of education among the slaves. The crime of teaching a slave to read is punishable with severe fines and imprisonment, and, in some instances, with *death itself*.[6]

About a million and a half people were kept in slavery in the United States when Douglass was born. By the time he escaped, 20 years later, this number had risen to two and a half million, concentrated largely in the Deep South states between Louisiana and Georgia. Upper South states like Maryland had a reputation for practicing a less severe form of slavery than the cotton and sugar plantations of the Deep South, with more opportunities for interaction between the races and milder discipline. But the masters on the Lloyd plantations where Douglass lived were also said to be crueler than most. Whatever its form, slavery remained—despite the pretensions of the master class—a system by which physical labor was brutally extracted from a distinct group of people through the persistent violation of their individuality.[7]

Abolitionist Senator Charles Sumner once said that the "single object" of slavery was "to compel labor without wages."[8] Modern slavery scholar Orlando Patterson defines slavery as "social death."[9] But it would be more precise to say that the master aimed to transform the slave into an automaton by obliterating his sense of personhood. "Freedom of choice is the essence of all accountability," Douglass wrote. Therefore, to make a man a slave, one must first "rob him of moral responsibility."[10] To accomplish that goal, the masters had to deny slaves at least three things: history, law, and the fruits of their labor.

History is a shared tradition about one's origins and the glorification of the achievements of ancestors, which gives one a sense of purpose and a role in the progress of the world. History can generate pride and solidarity among a people. Enforced illiteracy and propaganda kept history away from slaves, leaving them with only oral traditions and family histories that the master class regarded as quaint or ridiculous. This history-deprivation also bred among slaves a sense of being "pegged down to one single spot." Lacking a conception of their part in the progress of a nation or a people, enslaved people were encouraged to regard themselves not as dynamic and full of potential, but as static and fixed in the landscape. If the slave could be deprived of a past, he could not imagine a future. "The enthusiasm which animates the bosoms of young freemen, when they contemplate a life in the far West, or in some distant country," Douglass wrote, "could have no place in the thought of the slave."[11] This reticence to travel obviously served the interests of the master class.

Depriving slaves of law was also essential. Law establishes consistent rules that are mutually obeyed by ruler and ruled alike. Unlike a system of command-and-obedience, law gives shelter to the underprivileged, since the powerful must submit to it, and the powerless can use it to effectuate their own desires. Slaves were almost universally denied standing to invoke law, on the theory that, as the North Carolina Supreme Court frankly

5

explained, "[t]he slave, to remain a slave, must be made sensible, that there is no appeal from his master; that his power is in no instance, usurped; but is conferred by the laws of man at least, if not by the law of God." For courts or government officials to regard the slave as a legally independent being would "chang[e] the relation in which these parts of our people stand to each other."[12] To be truly subjugated, the slave had to be law-starved. Even such relatively innocuous matters as legal recognition of marriage might have tied a master's hands.

The lawless quality of slavery descended even to the plantations themselves, which operated less on the basis of strict and scrupulously followed protocols than through arbitrary and vague edicts. Indefinite or ambiguous rules give the enforcer discretion to punish whatever and whenever he likes. "A mere look, word, or motion,—a mistake, accident, or want of power,—are all matters for which the slave may be whipped at any time," wrote Douglass. A slave could even be punished for being too diligent. "Does he answer *loudly*, when spoken to by his master, with an air of self-consciousness? Then, he must be taken down a button-hole lower, by the lash."[13] Slaves found various strategies to compensate for this deprivation—folk customs, poetry and humor, and traditions like jumping the broom. But as much comfort as these gave, they were inadequate compared with the persistent lawlessness of their condition.

Eradicating the profit motive also flowed from the logic of slavery: slaves were property, so it made no sense to say they themselves could own property. But depriving them of opportunities for profit also rendered it impossible for them to plan for the future, prevented them from becoming economically independent, stifled a crucial source of self-esteem, and suppressed the incentive to undertake their own projects—all of which might prove dangerous to masters. Slaves were sometimes even punished for suggesting better ways to accomplish plantation tasks. Although denying slaves rewards for hard work or initiative was economically inefficient (it discouraged invention and entrepreneurialism), that inefficiency was a price plantation owners were willing to pay.[14] Slavery was productive enough to satisfy the master class. And thanks to property restrictions on voting and legislative malapportionment, it was the masters who made the important political decisions. Plus, the economic outlook for slavery began to improve when the cotton gin was invented and new western lands were opened for cultivation with the purchase of Louisiana in 1803.

In any event, slavery was not really about economics, at least not to the masters, who professed to scorn the materialism and profit-seeking of their capitalist Yankee cousins. America's founding fathers had generally viewed slavery as a regrettable institution or a necessary evil, but the first generation of southerners after the Constitution came to see slavery as a matter of nationalism and even humanitarianism. South Carolina's John C. Calhoun, the arch champion of slavery, called it a "positive good" because it provided the best life for those he saw as racially inferior and gave the master race leisure for the finer pursuits. Southerners "fancy themselves more generous and noble-hearted than the plain freemen who labour for subsistence," wrote John Quincy Adams in his diary after an 1820 conversation with Calhoun, but this was mere "vain-glory in their very condition of masterdom."[15]

While most southern whites could afford no slaves, or very few, even poor whites could benefit psychologically by being able to feel themselves part of the master race. Thus, during the three decades before the Civil War, southerners concocted a culture of pseudo-chivalry, heavily influenced by romantic authors like Sir Walter Scott. Plantation owners fancied themselves lords and ladies, commoners played faithful yeomen or flamboyant soldiers, and questions of filthy lucre were disregarded as beneath one's notice. Southerners, Adams concluded, "look down on the simplicity of a yankey's [*sic*] manners because he has no habits of overbearing like theirs, and cannot treat negroes like dogs."[16] According to Kenneth Stampp, one of the leading scholars of slavery, the institution is best seen not as an economic model but as "a social pattern made venerable by long tradition and much philosophizing." For those who were "emotionally and ideologically committed to the agrarian way of life" and to the "idea that those who lived on the land were more virtuous than those who engaged in commerce and industry," slavery was highly efficient and a powerful tool for satisfying the lust for domination—a commodity forever in demand.[17]

One epigone of that lust was Captain Aaron Anthony. Relatively speaking, he was not a particularly severe overseer, but he and his family were emblematic of the system. Douglass's first encounter with the absolute power whites had over blacks came when he witnessed Anthony beating his teenaged aunt Esther Bailey, who "possessed that which was ever a curse to the slave girl—namely, personal beauty."[18] Anthony was infatuated with her—Douglass does not disclose what exactly their connection was, if any—and ordered her not to see Ned Roberts, a young enslaved man she liked. She and Roberts, of course, could not marry, but they continued to meet in secret. When Anthony caught them, he flew into a rage. He stripped Esther to the waist, tied her hands over a beam in the cooking shed, and beat her bloody with a three-foot club made of cowhide. Seven-year-old Frederick, watching through a crack in a wall, never forgot her screams.

Overseers like Anthony, and the subordinates who helped him maintain order, were generally kept at arm's length by the genteel class of southerners, who regarded them with a mixture of fear and contempt but could not do without them. Among the strictest was Orson (or Austin) Gore, one of the Lloyd family's overseers. Gore was a swaggering, cool, unapproachable man, a true-born tyrant with "a stern will, an iron-like reality."[19] On one occasion in 1823, he began whipping a young man named Bill Denby. When Denby tried to flee, Gore drew a pistol, gave him the count of three, and then calmly shot him through the head.

Anthony and Colonel Lloyd protested, but Gore answered that such severe methods were essential to discipline, and the matter was dropped. Murder with impunity was not uncommon on the plantations.[20]

More common, however, were those ordinary interactions through which human sympathy might briefly shine, only to have the window slam shut again, thus emphasizing the impenetrable barrier between black and white, slave and free. That seems to have happened often in Douglass's relationship with the Auld family: Aaron Anthony's daughter Lucretia, her husband Thomas Auld, Thomas's brother Hugh, and his wife Sophia. Lucretia took a motherly interest in young Frederick. When Aunt Katy's stinginess left him famished, he would sing beneath her window, and she would toss him a slice of bread. When a bully hit him in the head with a rock, she brought him into the parlor and bandaged him.

In 1826, Anthony fell ill—he died only months later—and Lucretia stood to inherit part of his estate, including ownership of Frederick. Biographer William McFeely argues that it was her idea to send Douglass to Baltimore to live with Hugh and Sophia.[21] It is impossible to know for sure. While Douglass later acknowledged the kindness of some members of the family, he saw no reason to believe the Baltimore trip was meant as a favor. Nonetheless, it was in Hugh and Sophia's home that he found the stability and opportunity he eventually transformed into freedom. The move thus turned out to be "one of the most interesting and fortunate events of my life."[22]

Douglass's feelings toward the Aulds always bore the tinge of a betrayed child. Their family stood on the other side of the glass, close enough to make clear how distant they and their affections really were. Slavery mimicked family life to the masters' satisfaction, with paternal owners professing to care for their childlike charges. But true warmth remained infinitely beyond reach—the same unbridgeable gap that separated Esther's love for Ned Roberts from Anthony's lust for her, or the compassion of Frederick's mother from the grudging superintendence of Aunt Katy. The master–slave relationship was a façade stretched over a compulsory—and therefore abhorrent—union, one motivated by advantage rather than care and in which every apparently sincere feeling was ultimately unreliable because it resulted from force rather than love.

The depth and brilliance of Douglass's prose when he wrote of these experiences leaves the reader with the unmistakable impression that the worst of slavery's many cruelties was that it deprived the enslaved of a real family. One famous passage of his memoirs makes clear the bitterness with which he abhorred—yet could never forget—the diabolical facsimile of home life that slavery presented to the world. The experience that more than anything "served to deepen my conviction of the infernal character of slavery, and to fill me with unutterable loathing of slaveholders," he wrote, was "their base ingratitude to my poor old grandmother."[23] Douglass painted a picture of her fate:

> She had served my old master faithfully from youth to old age. She had been the source of all his wealth; she had peopled his plantation with slaves; she had become a great grandmother in his service. She had rocked him in infancy, attended him in childhood, served him through life, and at his death wiped from his icy brow the cold death-sweat, and closed his eyes forever. . . . [H]aving outlived my old master and all his children, having seen the beginning and end of all of them, and her present owners finding she was of but little value, her frame already racked with the pains of old age, and complete helplessness fast stealing over her once active limbs, they took her to the woods, built her a little hut, put up a little mud-chimney, and then made her welcome to the privilege of supporting herself there in perfect loneliness. . . . The hearth is desolate. The children, the

unconscious children, who once sang and danced in her presence, are gone. She gropes her way, in the darkness of age, for a drink of water. Instead of the voices of her children, she hears by day the moans of the dove, and by night the screams of the hideous owl. All is gloom. The grave is at the door. . . . She stands—she sits—she staggers—she falls—she groans—she dies—and there are none of her children or grandchildren present, to wipe from her wrinkled brow the cold sweat of death, or to place beneath the sod her fallen remains. Will not a righteous God visit for these things?[24]

Thomas Auld later claimed that this was untrue; he had treated Betsey Bailey relatively well in her old age. Douglass added a corrective footnote to his memoirs to acknowledge this—but he kept the story in his book just the same, suggesting that he may have mistrusted Auld's explanation. Certainly he had reason to doubt Auld's veracity in general.[25]

Still, while Douglass lamented being deprived of a family, there is one sense in which this deprivation may have been a blessing. Among the masters' most powerful tools was their hold over their slaves' relatives. In his own memoir of escape, the fugitive William Wells Brown wrote movingly of how the idea of being separated from his mother and siblings deterred him for a long time from running away. "If I could only have been assured of their being dead, I should have felt satisfied," he wrote. When he finally did run away, "the love of a dear mother, a dear sister, and three dear brothers yet living, caused me to shed many tears."[26] Even two decades after his own escape, Douglass wrote of his feelings at being "separated from all the dear ones of my youth as if by the shadow of death."[27] But at the time, being already separated from his family may have made it easier for him to flee. "Thousands would escape from slavery who now remain," wrote Douglass later, "but for the strong cords of affection that bind them to their families."[28] In fact, when Douglass's own aunt and uncle ran away in 1825, the master retaliated by selling their children south the very next day.[29]

In any event, Douglass never rested his condemnation of slavery on his own personal experience of it, but on its violation of universal moral principles. He recognized that to focus only on his own suffering when speaking out against slavery would in the end weaken his argument in the face of those who claimed that the cruelties he endured were the rare exception, and that most masters were humane. When he joined the abolitionist movement and began his career of public speaking, he was initially instructed to confine his comments to his own experiences rather than the moral and political principles represented by the institution of slavery. But he found he could not do this. It did not matter, he realized, whether a master was brutal or kind, or whether an enslaved person worked in a field or a house: slavery was, in any event, an outrage and a crime that could not be justified or rationalized. Even as a young man, his restless curiosity was constantly probing for fundamental truths to explain the episodes of his life. Something within him inevitably demanded to know: "Why am I a slave? Why are some people slaves and others masters?"[30] And he knew that the same longing for freedom pulled at the heart of every slave, no matter the conditions of their confinement. "Slavery is *itself* an abuse," he wrote. "It lives by abuse, and dies by the absence of abuse."[31]

# 2. Baltimore: 1826–1835

Baltimore was the second most populous city in the United States when eight-year-old Douglass moved in with Hugh and Sophia Auld. Along with about 80,000 residents, the city saw countless visitors and immigrants from many races and nations, and the Auld home in the shipbuilding neighborhood of Fell's Point was at its center. Hugh Auld was an ambitious naval carpenter preparing to start his own shipbuilding business. Twenty-nine-year-old Sophia was a kind mother and an inexperienced slave-mistress.

Douglass's portrayal of her in his memoirs illustrates how slavery's "fatal poison of irresponsible power"[1] could corrupt individual conscience by rewarding the worst instincts and punishing the best, in whites as well as blacks. Sophia's treatment of him was at first not merely kind, but sweet, motherly, and loving. Her warm home and gentle manner stoked the longing for family in the young boy. And she seems to have felt a desire to nurture him as she already cared for her two-year-old son Thomas.

His curiosity aroused by seeing Sophia read the Bible, Douglass asked her to teach him. Naively, she agreed. He caught on rapidly, and Sophia was proud enough of her student to mention his progress to Hugh. He exploded. Literacy, he cried, would "spoil the best nigger in the world," and "unfit him to be a slave."[2] If Frederick could read, he could also write, and that would inevitably lead to him running away. Abashed, Sophia instantly halted the lessons. But for young Frederick, Hugh's tirade was so obviously evil that in retrospect he considered it "the first decidedly *anti*-slavery lecture to which it had been my lot to listen," and it "stirred up" in his heart "a rebellion not soon to be allayed."[3]

But if this was a glimpse of light for him, it was also the first step toward the darkening of Sophia's spirit. "In ceasing to instruct me, my mistress had to seek to justify herself *to* herself."[4] Seeking to be a worthy wife, mother, and slave mistress, she turned against Frederick and flew into a rage whenever she spotted him peeking at a book. Yet it was too late to stop his curiosity. When left alone, he copied her son's schoolwork and devised a *Tom Sawyer*–like strategy for recruiting neighborhood children to help him learn. "When I met with any boy who I knew could write, I would tell him I could write as well as he. The next word would be, 'I don't believe you. Let me see you try it.' I would then make the letters which I had been so fortunate as to learn, and ask him to beat that. In this way I got a good many lessons."[5]

Hugh Auld was wise to fear slave literacy. Reading could kindle in a slave a desire for learning and for a personal future, thus undermining slavery's consistent effort to stamp out any sense of self-worth. A slave who could write could also forge one of the passes slaves needed when traveling without an escort, and use it to escape north. There was also the risk of abolitionist ideas. In 1829, a free-born black man in Massachusetts named David Walker published a pamphlet commonly called *Walker's Appeal*, denouncing slavery in emphatic terms. Only a few years later, it was widely—though, it seems, falsely—blamed for the bloody rebellion of some 70 Virginia slaves under the leadership of Nat Turner. White southerners instantly saw the peril of anti-slavery pamphlets and newspapers that put ideas into the heads of their captives, and so they banned such writings.

We know little of Douglass's daily life between his first taste of literacy around 1827 and the next great step in his life—when he purchased a copy of *The Columbian Orator* in 1831. Those years, however, witnessed some sensational conflicts over slavery in Baltimore, sparked by the vanguard abolitionist Benjamin Lundy and his protégé, William Lloyd Garrison. Lundy had been publishing his weekly *Genius of Universal Emancipation* since arriving in the city in 1825. The following spring, an infamous slave trader named Austin Woolfolk beat Lundy nearly to death on a Baltimore street after he denounced Woolfolk in the *Genius* as a "monster in human shape," and an "adamantine creature."[6] The slave dealer was convicted of attempted murder, but the jury imposed a fine of only $1. A year later, Lundy and Garrison published an attack on two other slave traders, damning them as "enemies of their own species—highway robbers and murderers."[7] Their targets sued for libel and won, but Garrison refused to pay the substantial fine, and was jailed for a month and a half. He continued to issue anti-slavery pamphlets and poetry from his cell.

Thus, young Douglass often heard the word "abolitionist" uttered bitterly by Hugh Auld and his friends, as they discussed the controversies roiling the city. But he claimed afterward that it was not until 1831 that he learned the meaning of the word, and that year was a pivotal one for the slavery controversy. It was the year of Nat Turner's rebellion. It was also the year Garrison began publishing *The Liberator*, which would become the most prominent of all anti-slavery newspapers. Also in 1831, John C. Calhoun issued his "Fort Hill Address," which articulated his theory of secession, and John Quincy Adams began introducing petitions against slavery in Congress.[8] When Southern representatives tried to keep such petitions out of the House of Representatives, abolitionists began organizing to send more.

As Douglass recalled it, newspaper reports about the petitions were his introduction to the world of abolitionism. He devoured the articles with "a deep satisfaction in the thought that the rascality of slaveholders was not concealed from the eyes of the world, and that I was not alone in abhorring the cruelty and brutality of slavery."[9] But his eyes were truly opened when he bought a copy of *The Columbian Orator*, an anthology of articles, poems, and dialogues intended as a schoolbook. Its editor, Caleb Bingham, included several selections targeting the evils of slavery in hopes of influencing young readers; in Douglass's case, at least, it worked.

The selection that made the greatest impression on him was "Dialogue between a Master and Slave," in which a slave explains his reasons for trying to run away in words so eloquent that they persuade the master to free him. "It is impossible to make one, who has felt the value of freedom, acquiesce in being a slave," says the enslaved character. When the master replies that slavery is an old institution, for which he is not at fault, the slave is unpersuaded: "The robber who puts a pistol to your breast may make just the same plea. Providence gives him a power over your life and property; it gave my enemies a power over my liberty. But it also gives me legs to escape with; and what should prevent me from using them? Nay, what should restrain me from retaliating the wrongs I have suffered, if a favorable occasion should offer?"[10]

*The Columbian Orator* did more than inspire in Douglass a passion for liberty. It taught him to view slavery as wrong in principle—not merely a personal fate, but a systematic evil. He could understand Sophia's behavior now. Her mistreatment of him was not just a flaw of character, but a manifestation of the perverse forces of slavery itself. The system, not Sophia alone, was responsible for his suffering and that of his fellow captives. "It was *slavery*, not its mere *incidents*, that I hated. . . . We were both victims to the same overshadowing evil, *she* as mistress, I as slave."[11]

The book and the newspapers also introduced Douglass to the rhetorical techniques of high romanticism. This style emphasized wit, classicism, elaborate imagery, and allusions to literature, especially scripture. It was also rich in elegy and invective. In the hands of abolitionist writers it could come off as syrupy—as in the case of Harriet Beecher Stowe's novel *Uncle Tom's Cabin*—or shrill—as in Garrison's *Liberator* articles, which damned slavery with vehement references to piracy, rape, and murder, all printed with exclamation points, italics, and all caps. Even reading this rich style of writing might baffle a reader who lacked formal education. To master this kind of expression, so as to express oneself vividly but without excessive melodrama or obscurity, required intense study and attention to detail. Douglass ultimately accomplished this with no schooling at all. He learned the power of language, and his profit on it was that he learned to curse slavery.

But his theft of education was interrupted in 1833, when a family quarrel led to him being sent back to Thomas Auld, who lived in St. Michaels, about a hundred miles from Baltimore. The move made the 15-year-old Douglass miserable. Thomas Auld was "destitute of every element of character capable of inspiring respect," and "incapable of a noble action."[12] Once again, Douglass was kept hungry. He began to steal food. He looked to religion for comfort and took hope when Auld professed a conversion to Methodism after a revival meeting. But Douglass soon found that his master saw his religious beliefs as a reason to treat his slaves even worse. "If religion had any effect on his character at all, it made him more cruel and hateful."[13]

This was an important discovery in what would become Douglass's complicated relationship with Christianity. His first experience of religious training had been in the primitive school at Wye House, where he memorized Bible verses on pain of whipping. Later, in Baltimore, a black preacher called "Uncle" Charles Lawson noticed his intelligence and talent for self-expression, and gave him the idea of becoming a preacher himself. Douglass evidently found the idea attractive, because he had defied Master Hugh's ban on attending Uncle Lawson's classes. Now in St. Michaels, the hysteria following the Nat Turner revolt led local whites to forbid blacks from meeting together, and as a consequence Douglass was barred from participating in a Sunday school where he had been teaching other slaves to read. Yet the nation's Protestant culture demanded Biblical literacy as the price of blessings in life and salvation after death. To keep slaves illiterate struck Douglass as positively sinful.

But there was more. It seemed obviously hypocritical for a professed Christian like Auld to hold other human beings in bondage at all, let alone to tyrannize over them. The rationalization—that

masters deprived their charges of freedom for their own good—
was a pathetic excuse for violating the liberty God gave every living being. And it was plainly false. Auld was a cruel man, who
sometimes whipped Douglass's crippled cousin Henny for not
moving fast enough. Nor was he unique in this. Another slave
owner who lived nearby, Reverend Rigby Hopkins, was notorious for beating his slaves every week, for trumped-up offenses,
simply to instill fear in them. Nonetheless, his white neighbors
admired Reverend Hopkins for his evangelism.

The churches were generally conservative regarding slavery,
if not active supporters of it. Clergymen and sometimes even
church corporations owned slaves. Southern preachers often actively supported slavery by quoting scripture, with the approval
of ecclesiastical authorities. Later in life, Douglass would often
dramatize this point by parodying the sermons in which southern clergymen exhorted slaves to bear their burdens unquestion-
ingly. Anti-slavery groups like the Quakers were shunned or ignored as a radical fringe. More mainstream sects that opposed
slavery in principle often did little to actively oppose it, or even
temporized their opposition, as did the Catholic Church, which
denounced the slave trade, but not slavery itself. Not until the
1840s would the Methodists and Baptists split into pro-slavery
southern and anti-slavery northern factions. Even then, northern
churches often segregated services. In 1838, Douglass stormed
out of a chapel in New Bedford, Massachusetts, when the pas-
tor administered the Eucharist first to white, and then to black
parishioners.

During his later career as an abolitionist orator, Douglass was
often exceptionally harsh in denouncing American congregations
for supporting, or silently accepting, slavery. He was especially
severe in *My Bondage and My Freedom*, the revised version of his
memoirs that he published in 1855. The "overwhelming mass
of professed Christians in America," he claimed, were hypocrites
and Pharisees, who "strain at a gnat and swallow a camel."[14]

Northern churchgoers who would refuse communion with a man who stole livestock would welcome a man who stole human beings—and would castigate abolitionists as fanatics and agitators. He could not understand how Christians could find cause to temporize or hesitate on a question as clear as slavery, and he could not abide their moral cowardice.

Years later, Booker T. Washington wrote that Douglass's religious beliefs were "not strictly orthodox," and that his early Methodist views "underwent a radical change" thanks to his experiences with slavery—particularly his life with Thomas Auld.[15] As an older man, Douglass rejected faith in the supernatural and embraced instead a secular belief in what he called the "absolute, inflexible law, moral and spiritual," discoverable by reason and applicable to all people. This moral law "accepts no excuses, grants no prayers" but governs human happiness and morality the way rules of nutrition and exercise govern man's physical health.[16] In any case, after his time with Auld, he never again had faith in the nation's Christian establishment.

The big transformation came the following year, in 1834, when Auld, fed up with "the boldness with which I defended myself against his capricious complaints," dispatched Douglass to Edward Covey, the notorious slave-breaker to whom exasperated masters would entrust troublemakers in need of taming.[17] Covey's 400-acre farm, appropriately called Mt. Misery, was in some ways a precursor of 20th-century reeducation and labor camps, and Covey's tactics of domination were a rudimentary form of the methods that the Nazis and Soviets later refined and mass-produced. Aleksandr Solzhenitsyn, Hannah Arendt, and other scholars have detailed how the 20th-century gulags used a mix of lying, isolation, disorientation, humiliation, "psychological contrast" (the good cop/bad cop method), and capricious rewards and punishments to destroy the inmates' sense of order and any possibility of psychological independence.[18] Covey employed all of these techniques in his efforts to break the spirits of those sent to him. Since only total subjugation could make slave labor productive, masters sought to inculcate a sense of utter domination in their human property. "Absolute power," writes the French sociologist Pierre Bourdieu, "is the power to make oneself unpredictable and deny other people any reasonable anticipation, to place them in total uncertainty by offering no scope to their capacity to predict."[19] Covey instilled that sense of bewilderment and terror in slaves by monitoring their every act and ensuring that they could never know what the master would do to them next.

Thus, he beat Douglass weekly, for infractions real or imagined. He forced Douglass to labor in the fields in all kinds of weather—rain, snow, hail—and sent him on errands he could not possibly perform—handling oxen, for instance, for which he had no training. When he inevitably failed, Covey punished him with the lash. He spied on Douglass, sneaked up on him, and ambushed him simply to drill into his mind the idea that the master might be watching at any time. Equally terrible was the experience of isolation: aside from Covey and his family, the farm consisted of only Douglass and two other workers. So far away from anyone who knew him, Douglass was rendered fundamentally alone.

The passage in his memoirs in which he described these hellish days became famous as among his most eloquent. Mt. Misery, he wrote,

> stood within a few rods of the Chesapeake Bay, whose broad bosom was ever white with sails from every quarter of the habitable globe. Those beautiful vessels, robed in purest white, so delightful to the eye of freemen, were to me so many shrouded ghosts, to terrify and torment me with thoughts of my wretched condition. I have often, in the deep stillness of a summer's Sabbath, stood all alone upon the lofty banks of that noble bay, and traced, with saddened heart and tearful eye, the countless number of sails moving off to the mighty ocean. The sight of

these always affected me powerfully. My thoughts would compel utterance; and there, with no audience but the Almighty, I would pour out my soul's complaint, in my rude way, with an apostrophe to the moving multitude of ships:—

"You are loosed from your moorings, and are free; I am fast in my chains, and am a slave! You move merrily before the gentle gale, and I sadly before the bloody whip! You are freedom's swift-winged angels, that fly round the world; I am confined in bands of iron! O that I were free! O, that I were on one of your gallant decks, and under your protecting wing! Alas! betwixt me and you, the turbid waters roll. Go on, go on. O that I could also go! Could I but swim! If I could fly! O, why was I born a man, of whom to make a brute. The glad ship is gone; she hides in the dim distance. I am left in the hottest hell of unending slavery. O God, save me! God, deliver me! Let me be free! Is there any God? Why am I a slave? I will run away. I will not stand it. . . . I have only one life to lose. I had as well be killed running as die standing. Only think of it; one hundred miles straight north, and I am free! Try it? Yes! God helping me, I will. . . . . There is a better day coming."[20]

But the daily abuse eventually worked. After six months, Douglass was broken. "My natural elasticity was crushed; my intellect languished; the disposition to read departed, the cheerful spark that lingered about my eye died out; the dark night of slavery closed in upon me, and behold a man transformed to a brute!"[21]

He said no more about the internal psychological experience of being rendered a brute—it was impossible, he said, to describe what it felt like to be "completely wrecked, changed, and bewildered"[22]—but he often used the term "darkness" to describe the slave's daily life, and spoke of "the silence of annihilation—of mental and moral annihilation."[23] This was a life in which the only thing that mattered was "temporal well-being"[24]—a stupor in which the truly broken slave lost all sense of personal efficacy or self-possession. His mental horizon shrank to a point. Even to dream of the freedom of ships in the bay became an unimaginable luxury. The only reality was the moment and the task at hand. This was the state of psychological degradation that philosopher Hannah Arendt described as "living death": "The end result" of the totalitarian labor camp, she wrote, "is inanimate men, *i.e.*, men who can no longer be psychologically understood, whose return to the psychologically or otherwise intelligibly human world closely resembles the resurrection of Lazarus."[25]

Douglass's own Lazarus moment was shortly to come. One day, after Covey administered an especially savage attack, he tried the only thing he could think of: he fled Mt. Misery for St. Michaels, to beg Thomas Auld for mercy. Covey made little effort to stop him, and Douglass, bleeding and exhausted, walked for miles in the sun to reach Auld's home. But Auld—"*my brother in the church,*" Douglass emphasized—was unmoved. While initially shocked at Covey's cruelty, the "systematic tyranny of slavery" overcame any sympathetic feelings he may have felt, and he ordered Douglass to return.[26]

The walk back proved to be a spiritual awakening. Describing the moment in *My Bondage and My Freedom*, he switched to a dramatic present tense: "Well, now I am clear of Covey, and of his wrathful lash, for the present. I am in the wood, buried in its somber gloom and hushed in its solemn silence; hid from all human eyes; shut in with nature and nature's God."[27] He tries to pray, but cannot. "The sham religion which everywhere prevailed" makes that impossible; it had "cast in my mind a doubt upon all religion."[28] He began to reflect on the duplicity of Auld and Covey, who called themselves Christians—Covey even forced him to sing hymns every evening—but who in truth were petty thugs. He could hope for no mercy from his owner, no succor from his friends, no rescue from a kindly mother figure, and, it now appeared, no protection from Almighty God.

As he approached Mt. Misery, Douglass came across the home of an old acquaintance, a native African called Sandy Jenkins, who offered him a charm to ward off Covey's whippings: a root that, if Douglass wore it on his right side, would make it impossible for a white man to whip him. Douglass thought this "very absurd and ridiculous, if not positively sinful," but Jenkins persuaded him to try it. "'My book learning,' he said, 'had not kept Covey off me,' (a powerful argument, just then)."[29] The root, of course, proved useless. His hopes were raised at first, when the slave-breaker did not attack him immediately. But that was because it was a Sunday, and Covey, a devout Sabbatarian, did his beating only on weekdays. The next morning, Douglass returned to work, pitching hay in the barn, and Covey, "in his peculiar snake-like way," sprang upon him out of nowhere.[30]

Douglass turned. Wrapping his muscular hands around Covey's throat, he held the man still for a moment. "My religious views on the subject of resisting my master," says Douglass, in narrating this scene, "had suffered a serious shock, by the savage persecution to which I had been subjected, and my hands were no longer tied by my religion."[31] Helpless until now, he decided to help himself. He tossed Covey to the ground, and when Covey lunged again, threw him back a second time. Again and again, Douglass held off his assaults. He claimed afterward that he did not strike the man, but only parried his blows—"strictly on the defensive."[32] However that may be, he was determined no longer to be beaten. Covey called to other workers to aid in subduing the rebel, but they refused. When he summoned his cousin Hughes to help, Douglass punched Hughes so hard that he stumbled off, breathless.

Alone, Covey and Douglass squared off for two hours. When at last they were both exhausted, the slave-breaker tried to pretend he had won. "Now, you scoundrel, go to your work," he said, walking away. "I would not have whipped you half so hard if you had not resisted."[33] But he had not whipped Douglass at all, or even drawn blood. For the second half of his year with Covey, Douglass was not beaten. He had proven to himself that he retained something essential that could not be taken away. The experience "was a resurrection from the dark and pestiferous tomb of slavery, to the heaven of comparative freedom. I was no longer a servile coward. . . . I had reached the point at which I was *not afraid to die*. This spirit made me a freeman in *fact*, though I still remained a slave in *form*."[34]

This moment became the centerpiece of Douglass's own story. He told the tale time and again, to illustrate the basic theme of his life's efforts. Those who desired freedom had to prove themselves worthy of it by struggle and self-determination. To be fully human meant to command oneself and to hazard life for the reward of living. In a sense, the fight with Covey hardened him—rendering him less likely to compromise and making him uncomfortable with the pacifism that animated the Quaker abolitionists. But it also gave him a sense of seriousness and integrity that was all his own. He might be ordered about, could be beaten or even murdered, but at 16 years old, his *self* once again belonged to him, and it would always remain that way. "Bruised I did get, but the instance I have described was the end of the brutification to which slavery had subjected me."[35]

# 3. The Escape: 1835–1839

In January 1835, Douglass was rented out to William Freeland, who owned a run-down farm about three miles from St. Michaels. Freeland was a different kind of slave owner. He had a sense of honor, and although he could be temperamental, he was not cruel. This, however, only further stoked Douglass's desire to be free. "Beat and cuff the slave, keep him hungry and spiritless, and he will follow the chain of his master like a dog," but "give him a good master, and he wishes to become his own master."[1]

His Lazarus-like revival from the tomb of slavery started the seemingly inevitable progress toward liberation. He swore to himself that he would make a break for freedom within a year; and a few months later, he, along with Sandy Jenkins and four other slaves, fashioned a plan to sneak north on Chesapeake Bay in a canoe under the cover of night. At daybreak, they would take to the land and walk to Delaware. Douglass began forging passes for his companions.

Enlisting the help of fellow slaves was a tremendous risk. Slaveholders spared no effort to keep slaves separate from and suspicious of one another, to make it as hard as possible for them to unite against their oppressors. Slaves were under constant surveillance, and masters exercised an "astonishing proficiency" in detecting subtle clues about slaves' private thoughts.[2] If one seemed distracted or unusually serious or betrayed the slightest hint of a "mood out of the common way," the master's attention would be aroused. He might begin to ask questions, change the work schedule, move the slave from one place to another, or even beat him preemptively, to elicit a confession.[3] Of course, any slave caught seeking freedom was subject to savage punishment and would forever lose what little standing he might have in his owner's eyes. Masters rewarded those who revealed escape plots and, if a slave did escape, punished those who remained, to ensure that they discouraged each other from any further attempts. With all these barriers in place, running away had so little chance of success that it was virtually irrational to try; it was more often in the slaves' interest to dissuade each other from an attempt or to betray their fellows' secrets.

As the day set for the breakout drew near, Jenkins withdrew from the plot. The others held firm, with Douglass's prodding: if they gave in, they were cowards, he told them, and deserved to be slaves. But as the tension mounted, Douglass had a weird premonition that the game was up. The morning of the planned escape, he turned to Jenkins and cried, *"Sandy, we are betrayed!—* something has just told me so."[4] Minutes later, an armed patrol galloped onto the plantation and arrested the plotters. While the officers were subduing one of the men, Douglass had time to burn his forged pass.

The conspirators were dragged behind horses five miles to a jail in Easton, where all but Douglass were soon released. He remained alone in his cell for a week. His desolation once more became almost unbearable, as slave traders came to shop, inspecting the inmates as possible purchases. When at last Thomas Auld arrived to retrieve him, he announced that he planned to sell Douglass south—generally considered the severest punishment that could be inflicted on an enslaved person. Yet, Auld did not do this. Instead, he ordered the young man back to Baltimore, to live once more with Hugh and Sophia. It is not clear why he changed his mind, but it was an act of comparative mercy. "He had the power and the provocation to send me, without reserve, into the very Everglades of Florida," Douglass reflected, "and his refusal to exercise that power must be set down to his credit."[5] Indeed, it would prove to be Douglass's liberation.

Hugh Auld put the now 17-year-old Douglass to work as an apprentice caulker, building ships at Fell's Point. Biographer Dickson Preston discovered that the ships Douglass helped build were, ironically, slave transports.[6] It was rough work. White laborers often struck him for disobedience or mistakes. He tried to fight back but was outnumbered. Once, when a gang of toughs delivered a particularly savage beating, Auld went to the police to complain. "I am sorry," came the answer, "but I cannot move in this matter, except upon the oath of white witnesses."[7] Because the only people willing to testify about the crime were black, and the courts would not allow them to introduce evidence, Auld had no legal recourse for the damage to his property. The laws regarding slavery sometimes even stymied the owners.

Auld had a personal stake in the matter, of course: his slave's work in the shipyards was bringing him good money. Every payday, Douglass handed over his earnings. While Douglass preferred this work to the drudge labor of the countryside, it grated on him to give up his $9 each week to Hugh Auld. "I contracted for it, worked for it, collected it; it was paid to me, and it was rightfully my own; and yet upon every returning Saturday night, this money—my own hard earnings, every cent of it,— was demanded of me and taken from me by Master Hugh. He did not earn it; he had no hand in earning it; why, then should he have it? I owed him nothing."[8] This "practice of openly robbing me, from week to week"[9] somehow made slavery even more unendurable than it had been on the farm with the daily prospect of flogging. At first, he tried a bargain: he would rent out his own time and pay Auld $3 per week, in addition to paying for his room, board, and working tools, and Auld would let him keep the rest. Auld agreed, of course; it meant more money in his pocket. But it gave Douglass hope. Any money he could save was money he could spend either buying his own freedom or making good an escape plan. But the arrangement collapsed when he was late coming home one weekend, and Auld flew into a rage at him for not getting permission first. That was the last straw.

On September 3, 1838, Douglass, dressed in the uniform of a U.S. Navy sailor, and carrying government papers smuggled to him on the Underground Railroad, boarded the Negro Car on a train bound for Wilmington, Delaware. Approaching the Susquehanna River, the conductor came into the compartment, collecting tickets. Douglass's heart pounded as he watched him approach, scrutinizing the documents carried by the black passengers. He held out his hand to Douglass, who struck a bold pose and turned over his sailor's pass. It was the moment of truth: the written description on the pass did not match Douglass, and the game would be up if the conductor read it too carefully. But the man only gave it a perfunctory glance and moved along. The danger was still not over, even when the train reached Wilmington, for the border states were rife with slave-catchers and bounty-hunters, and Douglass saw several acquaintances he was sure would recognize him and blow his cover. Nevertheless, Douglass managed to evade suspicion as he caught a boat from Delaware to Philadelphia, and then a train to New York City. By the next morning, he was walking down Broadway.

He was awestruck by the prosperity of the metropolis. Having been taught that slavery was the basis of all wealth, he had assumed the North must be poor, and could hardly believe the bustling industry about him. He, however, was penniless. "I was indeed free—free from slavery, but free from food and shelter as well."[10] A stranger put him in touch with local members of the Underground Railroad. Given his shipbuilding skills, they decided the best place for him to go was New Bedford, Massachusetts, the capital of the whaling industry. There he could earn a living—not just for himself, but for his new wife, Anna Murray, a free black woman he had courted in Baltimore, and who now joined him in New York. After a quick wedding, they moved on to New Bedford, where they were taken in by a black abolitionist named Nathan Johnson.

At Johnson's suggestion, the couple adopted the surname "Douglass," borrowing it from a heroic character—"Black James Douglas," fighter for Scottish independence—in Walter Scott's immensely popular book-length poem "Lady of the Lake." The new name would help Douglass evade slave-hunters who might try to snatch him back to his owner in Maryland. But it was also a symbolic moment. Choosing his own name was one more step in the process of self-determination that represented true liberation from slavery. Adopting a new name, Booker T. Washington explained, "was one of the first signs of freedom" for those who escaped bondage.[11] The escaped slave William Wells Brown explained that he chose to call himself "William" instead of "Sandford," the name that "had been forced upon me," because he "detested the idea" of being known on his master's terms. While some freedmen used their masters' surnames when they obtained freedom, Brown wrote that he "would rather have adopted the name of 'Friday' and been known as the servant of some Robinson Crusoe, than to have taken his name."[12]

New Bedford was alive with railroads, factories, mills, and foundries, and Douglass was impressed by the difference between it and the relative indolence of Baltimore. Thrifty Yankees substituted machinery and animal labor for human drudgery. No time was wasted. Workmen were efficient and focused. "Everybody seemed in earnest."[13]

The same contrast struck the French traveler Alexis de Tocqueville, whose *Democracy in America* was being published at exactly this time. Sailing down the river between the free state of Ohio and the slave state of Kentucky, Tocqueville was impressed by the contrast between the different cultures of north and south. On the slavery side, it seemed as if "society has gone to sleep."[14] Whites associated manual labor with slavery and scorned industry. Instead, they aspired to a life of "idle ease."[15] In free Ohio, by contrast, "one will never see a man of leisure."[16] There, citizens saw "material well-being as the main object of [their] existence," and the opportunity for profit and self-improvement encouraged hard work and commerce.[17] This contrast was the clearest possible illustration, Tocqueville concluded, that slavery "not only prevents the white men from making their fortunes but even diverts them from wishing to do so."[18]

Douglass echoed these ideas in one of his most famous compositions, the lecture "Self-Made Men," which he wrote in the 1850s and delivered dozens of times to audiences all over North America. Freedom and social mobility, he argued, depended fundamentally on a culture that acknowledged the "respectability of labor"—that expected each person to provide for himself and rewarded honest toil rather than birth and privilege.[19] The industrial spirit and dynamism of the North was thus an active manifestation of the principle of equality, the principle that formed the basis—or ought to form the basis—of American values. Foreigners often remarked that Americans were in a constant state of agitation and excitement, "like the troubled sea," but that was just a testament to the national creed of equal freedom and self-reliance: because it liberated individuals to make their own choices, American society was more animated and alive than the static and class-oriented European nations. "Like the sea, we are constantly rising above and returning to, the common level."[20] This quality of American culture would become the fundamental link between Douglass's individualism and his patriotism. The U.S. Constitution was worthy of respect because its institutions regarded each individual as worthy of respect—or would, if its principles were faithfully implemented.

Immediately upon escaping from slavery, Douglass found that his new responsibilities filled him with a sensation of pride that he had never experienced before. Knowing he could reap the rewards of his own toil "placed me in a state of independence," he wrote, and his first day of freely chosen labor seemed to him "the real starting point of something like a new existence."[21]

> The fifth day after my arrival I put on the clothes of a common laborer, and went upon the wharves in search of work. On my way down Union street I saw a large pile of coal in front of the house of Rev. Ephraim Peabody, the Unitarian minister. I went to the kitchen-door and asked the privilege of bringing in and putting away this coal. "What will you charge?" said the lady. "I will leave that to you, madam." "You may put it away," she said. I was not long in accomplishing the job, when the dear lady put into my hand *two silver half-dollars*. To understand the emotion which swelled my heart as I clasped this money, realizing that I had no master who could take it from me—*that it was mine—that my hands were my own*, and could earn more of the precious coin—one must have been in some sense himself a slave. . . . I was not only a freeman but a free-working man, and no master Hugh stood ready at the end of the week to seize my hard earnings.[22]

Thus, Douglass viewed economic freedom as more than an incentive: it was the source and symbol of personal liberation. He made this idea explicit in a later speech: "What is freedom? It is the right to choose one's own employment. Certainly, it means that, if it means anything; and when any individual or combination of individuals undertakes to decide for any man when he shall work, where he shall work, at what he shall work, and for what he shall work, he or they practically reduce him to slavery. He is a slave."[23]

Douglass's feeling of pride at choosing his own employment was soured somewhat when white laborers on the wharves threatened to quit if the boss hired a black man. But, undeterred, he worked at a variety of odd jobs instead: sawing wood, digging cellars, unloading ships, moving barrels of whale oil, and helping cast brass at a foundry. "My hands," he wrote, were at long last "furnished with something like a leather coating."[24] As he labored, he also strove to improve his mind. He would nail a copy of William Lloyd Garrison's *Liberator* next to where he stood at the blacksmith's bellows and read it as he pumped the handles. He was free at last to take charge of his own life, as well as to provide for Anna and for their children, Rosetta, born in June 1839, and Lewis, born 16 months later. Three others would follow: Frederick Junior in 1842, Charles in 1844, and Annie in 1848.

In "Self-Made Men," Douglass celebrated the great thinkers and inventors who "are not brought up but who are obliged to come up, not only without the voluntary assistance or friendly co-operation of society, but often in open and derisive defiance of all the efforts of society and the tendency of circumstances to re-press, retard and keep them down."[25] The speech in no small degree reflected how Douglass liked to think of himself: self-made men, he wrote, "are in a peculiar sense, indebted to themselves for themselves . . . . If they have ascended high, they have built their own ladder."[26]

# 4. Joining the Cause: 1839–1845

In 1839, Douglass attended a lecture by William Lloyd Garrison, America's most prominent abolitionist. A spellbinding speaker and a revolutionary, Garrison denounced the Constitution of the United States for its compromises with slavery and, proclaiming the motto "no union with slaveholders," argued that northern states should secede from the Union to stop helping slavery persist. While his extremism attracted loyal followers, it also deterred many people who, though opposed to slavery, were unwilling to follow him in demanding an end to the United States itself. Advocates of slavery sometimes found Garrison a useful figure, an illustration of their view that abolishing the peculiar institution would also require the overthrow of American society.

By the time Douglass met him, Garrison's "ultra" position had already refashioned the politics of the abolition movement.[1] Opposition to slavery had been a feature of American life since the founding, but white Americans were generally stymied by the question of what to do with the slaves, once freed. Was it possible for them to remain in the United States? Thomas Jefferson, struggling with the question in his 1787 book *Notes on the State of Virginia*, had answered no: slaves and their descendants would never be able to forgive whites for slavery, and whites would find it impossible to let go of their racism. Freeing the slaves would therefore "produce convulsions which will probably never end but in the extermination of the one or the other race."[2]

One possible solution appeared in 1816 with the formation of the American Colonization Society, which proposed to establish a colony in Africa where freed slaves could go—or perhaps be sent. Jefferson supported the society, and his friend and successor James Madison served as its president. It did manage to start a colony in Liberia, the capital of which was named Monrovia after Jefferson's other society-supporting protégé, James Monroe. But the colonization effort was doomed from the start: over the course of its life, it arranged to move fewer than 20,000 people, compared with the total American slave population of more than 3 million. Worse, colonization was a moral outrage: most slaves had been born in America, had never visited Africa, and had no interest in going. Few had the skills needed to survive there. To deport them against their will was unconscionable—although there were plenty who wanted to try. Yet, its very futility and racism were what made colonization so attractive to many: it allowed upper-class whites to endorse anti-slavery principles, and thus appear humane, without actually taking steps to threaten the status quo. As Douglass later said, it "interpose[d] a physical impossibility between the slave and his deliverance," making it a politically safe position for white leaders.[3]

Garrison, more than any other figure, destroyed the respectability of the colonization movement and other moderate versions of opposing slavery. Railing against half-measures and thinly disguised racist schemes to send black Americans elsewhere, he insisted on "abolitionism" instead of colonization, which meant the immediate liberation of the slaves, without deportation, and without payment to slave owners. Masters claimed that the Constitution entitled them to be compensated if the government freed their slaves; but the new wave of abolitionists insisted that, if anyone deserved payment, it was the slaves themselves. They alone had suffered real deprivation.

Garrison's radicalism went beyond rejecting the idea of compensated emancipation. He denounced politics *in toto*. The U.S. Constitution was literally a deal with the devil, he said, because it protected slavery—and he burned it on stage during his speeches.

Not only was the Constitution irredeemably stained with the sin of slavery, but that sin corrupted the government entirely. To vote or serve in office was therefore to implicate one's own character and lend credibility to the slave-catching machine. Nor was violence a solution: Garrison was a pacifist. He was also a teetotaler, a feminist, and an anti-Sabbatarian, meaning he opposed Sunday closing laws and believed every day of the week to be the Sabbath.

Within the small world of anti-slavery politics, Garrison's denunciations of colonization won the day, and his American Anti-Slavery Society and its various state chapters took over leadership of the movement in the 1830s. Garrison became a celebrity, even if his actual influence on American politics remained relatively minor. Civil disobedience, nonviolent protest, and thunderous rhetoric were his tools. He was despised almost as much in the North as he was in the South. In 1835, he was nearly lynched, not in a slave state, but in Boston, Massachusetts, where an outraged mob dragged him through the streets with a rope tied around him. Three years later, a crowd in Philadelphia, infuriated by one of his speeches, torched Pennsylvania Hall, a grand edifice built for the purpose of holding abolitionist meetings, only three days after it was completed.

As anti-slavery activists grew more radical, so did the views of slavery's defenders. Southern leaders such as Jefferson or Madison had long regarded slavery as a curse, or as a historical aberration that Americans might outgrow. But the new generation now embraced slavery as a blessing—as a benefit to both slave and master. Slavery, they claimed, was a humane alternative to the industrial capitalism rising in Europe and in the northern states. Where capitalism was motivated by profit and greed and—to borrow a phrase from today's sociologists—treated people as atomistic individuals, slavery was a family-like social structure, which regarded each person as a whole being and in which each contributed to the collective welfare under the oversight of intelligent and beneficent masters. In his lengthy poem "The Hireling

35

and the Slave," South Carolina poet William Grayson bemoaned the fate of the worker in the free market:

> What blessing to the churl has freedom proved,
> What want supplied, what task or toil removed?
> Hard work and scanty wages still their lot. . . .

On the plantation, by contrast, the slave was

> Taught by the master's efforts, by his care
> Fed, clothed, protected many a patient year. . . .
> Guarded from want, from beggary secure,
> He never feels what hireling crowds endure,
> Nor knows, like them, in hopeless want to crave
> For wife and child, the comforts of the slave. . . .[4]

Among the most eloquent of slavery's advocates was Virginia's George Fitzhugh, whose 1854 book, *Sociology for the South, or, the Failure of a Free Society*, was astoundingly frank. Fitzhugh contrasted "economics," which was the study of a free society, with sociology, the study of the slave state.[5] Free society was dominated by individualism, or as Fitzhugh put it, "Every man for himself, and Devil take the hindmost." The slave state, on the other hand, was the "very best form of socialism,"[6] a communitarian ideal that elevated the welfare of the collective over the "presumptuous" and "infidel philosophy" of self-interest that was embodied in the phrase "the pursuit of happiness." Slavery was based on the premise that the individual has "no rights whatever, as opposed to the interests of society . . . . Whatever rights he has are subordinate to the good of the whole; and he has never ceded rights to it, for he was born its slave, and had no rights to cede."[7] Fitzhugh did not shy away from the suggestion that slavery was so desirable that it might also be a good idea to enslave whites.

These arguments were so brazen that Garrison almost welcomed them. He reprinted long passages in *The Liberator* to show the depths to which slavery's advocates were willing to descend. But many masters shared Fitzhugh's romanticized notion that slavery benefited and protected slaves. They saw slaves as primitive, childlike, subhuman, and therefore in need of the guidance and protection of whites. They viewed criticisms from northerners who did not live with slaves as ignorant meddling and answered reports of brutality with their own tales of benign owners and loyal, happy bondsmen. After Harriet Beecher Stowe fictionalized several real-life instances of masters' cruelty in *Uncle Tom's Cabin*, southern writers published fictionalized responses that portrayed slaves as content and infantile, and abolitionists as terrorists bent on stirring up violent insurrections. Testaments by escapees like Douglass were priceless evidence in efforts to refute the growing mythology of slavery as a "positive good."

Douglass attended anti-slavery meetings for three years in New Bedford and read every issue of *The Liberator*. He later wrote that he did not then consider becoming an abolition orator, but in a sense, he had been training for such an opportunity ever since he first read *The Columbian Orator*. Public speaking was not new to him: he had been teaching Sunday school classes for years already, and he began speaking before black audiences almost immediately after his escape to the North. He received a preaching license from the African Methodist Episcopal Zion Church in 1839 and, in March of that year, gave an address denouncing colonization. Given his zeal and his gift for expression, it was only natural that he would embrace an opportunity to play a part in the cause, despite the significant risks of doing so.

A new opportunity came in 1841, when a convention of some 1,000 attendees gathered in Nantucket, Massachusetts. He had never spoken before such a large crowd, but an activist who knew him from his classes asked him to tell his story. Garrison was prominently seated up front, and Douglass was awestruck.

"I trembled in every limb. I am not sure that my embarrassment was not the most effective part of my speech, if speech it could be called." But it was at least effective enough to inspire Garrison to seize the rhetorical opportunity. "Have we been listening to a thing, a piece of property, or to a man?" he called out when Douglass was finished. "A man!" the audience shouted back. "Shall such a man ever be sent back to slavery from the soil of old Massachusetts?" The crowed cried in unison, "No!"[8]

Impressed by Douglass's talk, Garrison and other leaders approached him after the meeting and invited him to speak at other gatherings in the future. Thus began his public career as an orator and activist. Years later, after he had repudiated Garrison's version of abolitionism, Douglass issued a revised edition of his memoirs in which he implied that Garrison and his supporters had been reluctant from the very beginning to let Douglass discuss in public the broader political and philosophical questions relating to slavery. "Give us the facts," he recalled one leader saying. "We will take care of the philosophy." But he could not follow that advice. "It was impossible for me to repeat the same old story month after month and keep up my interest in it. . . . I could not always follow the injunction, for I was now reading and thinking."[9]

While the Garrisonians may have revealed a degree of racial condescension in their effort to dissuade Douglass from discussing the broader theory of slavery and freedom, they were also concerned with ideological purity and political focus.[10] Small activist communities typically strive to maintain a single, consistent message in all public pronouncements, and they are often hypersensitive about dissension within their ranks. This was particularly true at the time Douglass joined the Garrisonians. Only a year before, they had suffered a shock when wealthy New York philanthropist Gerrit Smith broke from them and endorsed a *pro*-Constitution version of abolitionism that rejected their hostility to political, legal, or military action. The schism wounded the Garrisonians, and they feared that pro-slavery forces would take advantage of such internal squabbling. That experience likely made them reluctant to allow any newcomer, even Douglass, to speak unsupervised.

In the 1840s, Douglass was learning the skills of public speaking and writing, and it was natural for him to yield to the advice of his sponsors, even if he disagreed with them. But as he gained experience on the lecture circuit, he increasingly found himself telling the story of the battle with Edward Covey—the turning point in his life—and he made the story the climactic moment of his first great memoir, *Narrative of the Life of Frederick Douglass, An American Slave*, published in 1845. These violent passages inevitably jarred with the Garrisonians' pacifism, and scholar Robert Levine suggests that they reveal a "quietly subversive motif" in Douglass's writing.[11] This seems an exaggeration; Garrison himself considered it legitimate to use force in self-defense, and Douglass went out of his way, even in later revisions of his book, to claim that he had only tried to fend off Covey's attack. Still, when he wrote in the *Narrative* that the lesson he learned from the Covey fight was that "the white man who expected to succeed in whipping, must also succeed in killing me," there was more than a hint of his later militancy.[12]

In any event, Douglass stuck to the Garrisonian message, rejecting the Constitution and political involvement, and pledging nonviolence—despite being violently attacked during some of his lectures. "While you are in the Union, you are as bad as the slaveholder," he told an audience in 1845. "God says thou shalt not oppress: the Constitution says oppress: which will you serve, God or man?"[13] Summoning the rich eloquence of Victorian-era rhetoric, Douglass unloaded his venom on the United States as a slave society. "In thinking of America, I sometimes find myself admiring her bright blue sky—her grand old woods—her fertile fields—her beautiful rivers—her mighty lakes, and star-crowned mountains," he wrote in a letter to *The Liberator*. "But my rapture is soon checked, my joy is soon turned to mourning. When I remember that all is cursed with the infernal spirit of slaveholding, robbery and wrong,—when I remember that with the waters of her noblest rivers, the tears of my brethren are borne to the ocean, disregarded and forgotten, and that her most fertile fields drink daily of the warm blood of my outraged sisters, I am filled with unutterable loathing, and led to reproach myself that any thing could fall from my lips in praise of such a land."[14]

He would always relish the adventure and danger of the 1840s and 1850s, touring the United States, pronouncing radical denunciations of slavery's evils alongside his brother dissidents, often at great risk to himself. Many times he was egged or stoned at his speeches. In 1860, a Boston crowd nearly murdered him on stage. On another occasion, his hand was broken. Still another time, when he refused to yield his seat on the train to a white man, a mob tore the bench on which he was sitting from the floor of the car—an incident so violent that the railroad company ordered its engineers not to stop in the town where Douglass lived. His fondest recollections were of the ways white abolitionist brethren insisted on sharing in his deprivations, sitting with him in the Jim Crow cars on trains, or sleeping on the decks of steamboats if he was not allowed to sleep inside. "True men they were, who could accept welcome at no man's table where I was refused."[15]

Yet, as he traveled throughout the land, sharing stages with other abolitionists, he increasingly found himself cramped by the Garrisonians' party line. His "first offense against our Anti-Slavery Israel" came when he openly objected to a presentation by another abolitionist who sought to address the crowd not only about slavery, but also on the subject of communism.[16] It was distracting, Douglass thought, and likely to make listeners less receptive to the anti-slavery message. But rather than praising Douglass for staying on point, the abolitionist Maria Chapman, who served on the board of Garrison's Massachusetts Anti-Slavery Society, and always distrusted Douglass, rebuked him on the grounds that Gerrit Smith and other non-Garrisonians might make use of "my seeming rebellion against the commanders of our anti-slavery army."[17]

That was in 1843, and the dispute blew over. But in the years that followed, Douglass continued to buck at the strictures imposed by Garrisonian dogmatists. In the meantime, he got to know Smith and his allies. By this time, they had founded the nation's first openly anti-slavery political party, the Liberty Party. Smith and his allies claimed that the Constitution, if correctly interpreted, was a fundamentally *anti*-slavery document. Rejecting the Garrisonian taboos against political participation, they believed that abolitionists should *use* the nation's supreme law, rather than setting themselves against it. Along with Smith, radical lawyers such as Lysander Spooner, Joel Tiffany, and William Goodell began to publish books and monographs making that case, and Douglass began reading them in earnest.[18]

Garrison published Douglass's *Narrative* to wide acclaim in 1845. It was far from the only such testament by an escaped slave, but its simple, straightforward style and gripping episodes of brutality and liberation made it the most popular. Although it fell into neglect in the early 20th century, it has today taken its proper place among the classics of American autobiography. Douglass himself considered it a minor production. He was far prouder of the later editions, the bold *My Bondage and My Freedom* in 1855, and the more stolid *Life and Times of Frederick Douglass*, issued first in 1881, and in revised form in 1893.

The *Narrative* scandalized readers with its graphic descriptions of brutality and its hints at rape. Some slave owners and northern sympathizers protested what they called exaggerations, or even lies, and insisted that most masters were mild and patient, not the liars and thugs Douglass described. Abolitionists promptly backed up their accusations with proof. Yet, the *Narrative* went beyond merely describing events. However much the Garrisonians might have preferred that he confine himself to his own story, Douglass used his memoir to reflect on slavery's political and psychological nature.

Among its most memorable passages is that in which Douglass explains why masters encouraged slaves to drink during the Christmas holidays—"to disgust their slaves with freedom, by plunging them into the lowest depths of dissipation."[19] Another is his explanation of singing on plantations, a habit naive whites sometimes saw as proof that slaves were content. In truth, Douglass noted, they "sing most when they are most unhappy"[20]—their songs aimed to relieve sorrow, rather than express joy. Douglass also went beyond his personal experience with cutting denunciations of the churches that supported or tolerated slavery. "[T]he religion of the south," he wrote, "is a mere covering for the most horrid crimes," and northern churches were not much better.[21] In these passages and others, Douglass explored the sociology of slavery—one reason the Narrative has become an American classic.

But the Narrative's publication was also dangerous. Because Douglass named names and revealed so many details, it raised a real prospect that he might be captured by slave-hunters and returned to his master in Maryland. Friends recommended that he leave the country for a while to avoid the risk. His wife and children, being free, could remain behind, but that summer, Douglass departed for the free soil of Great Britain, where he spent the next year and a half lecturing against slavery and the American Constitution.

# 5. Great Britain and Conversion: 1845–1852

Trouble began for Douglass even before his ship arrived in Liverpool on August 28, 1845. As the steamer crossed the Atlantic, several passengers, having read copies of the *Narrative* that he distributed, asked him to lecture on slavery to help pass the time. But one clique of southerners loudly complained and swore they would throw Douglass overboard for his "lies." At last, the captain was forced to intervene and silence the protest, but the incident became known in England, where such violent prejudice was socially unacceptable—and that gave Douglass yet another opportunity to expound on the evils of racism.

While his British sojourn proved immensely successful for Douglass, relations between him and his Garrisonian sponsors became increasingly strained. Shortly after he arrived, he learned that Maria Chapman did not trust him to handle the group's money and even accused him of embezzlement. Douglass was indignant, but when he protested, Chapman interpreted his reaction as vanity, as did her friend Richard Webb, at whose home Douglass was staying. Webb called Douglass "by much the least loveable and the least easy of all the abolitionists. . . . I think his selfishness intense, his affections weak, and his unreasonableness quite extravagant when he is in the slightest degree hurt or when he thinks himself hurt."[1]

As with their earlier advice to confine himself to personal stories, these words have struck some as evidence of the Garrisonians' latent racism. Certainly they reflected an increasing suspicion of Douglass's intellectual independence. The Garrisonians were a tight-knit, slightly paranoid cadre of radicals, who habitually regarded even sympathetic critics as traitors to the cause, and they were all white. Douglass, meanwhile, had a jealous sense of his own individuality, borne of his hard-won recognition that personal pride was an essential quality of a free man. It was only natural that Quakers and other pacifists interpreted his sense of self-worth as "selfishness," and he had a temper that may have been too easily triggered. These differences of character and ideology played a role in his eventual break with Garrison and his followers.

As Douglass matured as a speaker and author, and addressed immense crowds every night, he was awed by the lack of race prejudice in Britain. "The people here know nothing of the republican negro-hate prevalent in our glorious land. They measure and esteem men according to their moral and intellectual worth, and not according to the color of their skin."[2] He also met with prominent European abolitionists, who did not share many of the Garrisonians' beliefs—particularly their refusal to vote or engage in politics. British political activists had achieved important successes by political means: abolishing slavery in the British West Indies, repealing the protectionist Corn Laws, and obtaining legislation favorable to Irish autonomy. All of this demonstrated the potential gains that the Garrisonians, by disavowing political participation, were giving up.

While in Europe, Douglass twice revised and republished the *Narrative*. The pamphlet's popularity brought him a measure of financial independence, and by perfecting his *Narrative*, Douglass was able to take control of his own life in an unusually literal fashion. Each of the two revisions hinted more strongly at his growing independence. In the second edition, published in Ireland in 1846, Douglass added a direct answer to a Maryland critic who claimed in the newspapers that the book libeled Edward Covey and Thomas Auld, and that Douglass could not have written the book because he was an illiterate slave. After calmly answering each charge, Douglass concluded that he was "a new man" since escaping from slavery. He may once have been a timid bondsman, but freedom had "given me a new life," and "[i]f I should meet you where I now am, amid the free hills of Old Scotland, where the ancient 'Black Douglass' once met his foes, I presume I might summon sufficient fortitude to look you full in the face." In fact, he threatened, "It may be that, wearing the brave name which I have assumed, might lead me to deeds which would render our meeting not the most agreeable. Especially might this be the case, if you should attempt to enslave me."[3]

This menacing language seemed once again to clash with Garrisonian pacifism. Yet, during his tour of Britain—some of which was spent happily in company with Garrison himself, who visited England in the last half of 1846—he articulated radical abolitionism in stirring terms. "[T]he entire network of American society, is one great falsehood, from beginning to end," he told one London audience. "In their celebrated Declaration of Independence, they made the loudest and clearest assertion of the rights of man; and yet at that very time the identical men who drew up that Declaration of Independence, and framed the American democratic constitution, were trafficking in the blood and souls of their fellow men." The Constitution "consecrates every rood of earth in that land over which the star-spangled banner waves as slave-hunting ground."[4] Asked whether Americans were not offended by his denunciation of their nation's highest law before British audiences, Douglass snapped back that he was "anxious to irritate the American people" on the subject of slavery. "The conscience of the American public needs this irritation. And I would *blister it all over from centre to circumference*, until it gives signs of a purer and a better life."[5]

His growing confidence and bold manner of speaking made him powerfully attractive to the women he met. He was a handsome man, tall, fit, with a deep voice and a fierce and striking face, set off by a dashing hairstyle that seemed straight out of the romantic novels he loved. "You can hardly imagine," wrote one breathless Garrisonian colleague, "how he is noticed,—*petted* I might say by *ladies*."[6] There is no proof that he had any romances with them, although it was during this time that he met Julia Griffiths, who became one of his closest friends—and possibly more—after his split with Garrison. But what evidence exists suggests that Douglass adhered rigidly to Victorian proprieties while in Britain. Abolitionists were often falsely accused of sexual misbehavior by those who assumed that their radicalism was proof of a dangerously anti-social mindset. Those like Garrison and Douglass, who broke taboos by advocating female suffrage and letting women speak at public meetings, were especially targeted by such smears. Added to that was the ever-present sexual anxiety that shrouded slavery itself. Blacks were often depicted as rapacious sexual fiends, lusting after white flesh.[7]

As Douglass's time in Britain came to a close at the end of 1846, his admirers presented him with a special gift: having collected the money to buy his freedom from Thomas Auld, they proudly handed Douglass his own deed of sale. The surprise itself was an additional benefit because, had they asked first, Douglass might have been put in a tight spot. Garrisonians objected to paying to free slaves, because it appeared to acknowledge the owner's asserted property right. "Some of my uncompromising anti-slavery friends," he wrote later, "were not pleased that I consented to it, even by my silence."[8] But Garrison himself defended the choice. It was better for the cause, he thought, that Douglass be safe from seizure upon his return to America.

Thus, Douglass arrived back on home soil in the spring of 1847, a celebrity and rather well off. British supporters had raised enough money to help him take the next step in his career: establishing his own newspaper. When he broached the idea, the Garrisonians objected. *The Liberator*, they said, was enough. Douglass yielded to their judgment at first, but toward the end of the year, he changed his mind: he would proceed with the project after all. Moving to Rochester, New York, he began publishing *The North Star* in December. Where Garrison printed his motto, "No union with slaveholders" on the masthead, Douglass printed, "Right is of no sex—truth is of no color—God is the father of us all, and all we are brethren," and later simply, "All rights for all."

Close to the Canadian border, Douglass's Rochester home became a stop on the Underground Railroad, and his family aided in the escape of perhaps 400 runaways during their time there.[9] Rochester was also much closer to the headquarters of the Gerrit Smith wing of anti-slavery than was his old home in Garrison's Massachusetts, and he soon began devoting columns in his paper to debates with the pro-Constitution abolitionists. Ultimately, it was Douglass who was persuaded. In May 1851, he announced his conversion: the Constitution, he now believed, was an anti-slavery document, and abolitionists should vote, run for office, and use politics to fight for their cause. Disgusted by this apparent sellout, the Garrisonians claimed Douglass's change of mind was influenced by Smith's subsidies to *The North Star*—soon renamed *Frederick Douglass' Paper*. But there is no reason to believe the change was anything but sincere. Douglass was never afraid to differ respectfully but openly with his allies.

Smith and other anti-slavery constitutionalists began with the premise that the Constitution must be interpreted strictly in terms of its language, rather than the Founding Fathers' subjective intentions. What the Constitution's authors *meant* is not the law; what the Constitution actually *says* is. Thus, when the Constitution refers to "We the People of the United States," the word "people" must include black Americans, since nothing in the document says otherwise. "Neither in the preamble nor in the body of the Constitution is there a single mention of the term *slave* or *slave holder*," Douglass explained in an 1857 address. "'We the people'—not we, the white people, not we, the citizens or the legal voters—not we, the privileged class and excluding all other classes but we, the people."[10]

The anti-slavery constitutionalists emphasized a longstanding legal principle, holding that all laws that restrict natural rights must be interpreted as narrowly as possible, and that any time the meaning of a law is unclear, courts should interpret it in a way that will maximize freedom. These rules, combined with the broad purposes mentioned in the preamble—"to secure the blessings of liberty" and "ensure domestic tranquility"—meant the Constitution should be understood whenever possible as limiting slavery. In addition, several clauses seem directly contrary to slavery— the prohibition on bills of attainder, for instance, of which slavery is arguably one type, or the Fifth Amendment's promise that no person shall be deprived of liberty without due process of law. Other amendments guarantee fair trials and prohibit arbitrary seizures of persons or property. Given that slavery conflicted with these protections for freedom, the anti-slavery constitutionalists argued that the burden of proof was on defenders of slavery to show some foundation in the law for a practice that took freedom from people who had committed no crime. Absent some explicit justification for slavery in the Constitution, they believed that courts should at least presume against its legality.

Not only was slavery not expressly protected by the Constitution, Smith and his allies believed it was implicitly prohibited. They pointed to a sentence in article 4 of the Constitution that prohibits states from interfering with the "privileges and immunities of citizens of the United States." "Privileges and immunities" is a centuries-old legal term referring to personal freedoms. If black Americans were, indeed, citizens of the United States, then these words meant that states could have no power to deprive black American citizens of their liberty. Slavery's defenders, of course, argued that slaves were not and could never be American citizens and therefore had no privileges or immunities.

Chief Justice Roger B. Taney had even written an official memo taking this view while serving as Andrew Jackson's attorney general in the 1830s. The Constitution's authors, he wrote, had never contemplated black citizenship; they had intended to create a white nation. Thus, even black people who had never been slaves could not become American citizens.[11]

But nothing in the Constitution addressed the question explicitly. Indeed, the document never defined the word "citizen," which considerably complicated matters. Without such a definition, federal citizenship was assumed to spring automatically from citizenship in a state—individuals were federal citizens if and only if a state government recognized them as citizens. This created a problem because different states had different criteria for citizenship. Some drew no racial distinctions—a person of any race could be a citizen of Massachusetts, for instance, and consequently of the United States—but others, such as South Carolina, denied all black people recognition as citizens, whether born free or not. Thus, a person might be a U.S. citizen in some states but not in others—which was absurd, given that the "privileges and immunities" clause was written to bar states from making that type of distinction. When South Carolina adopted its "Negro Seaman's Act," which mandated that black sailors on any ship pulling into one of the state's ports be jailed until the ship departed, Massachusetts leaders argued that the act violated the "privileges and immunities" of black Massachusetts citizens who traveled on those ships. South Carolina ignored the complaints.

Smith and other anti-slavery thinkers argued that the privileges and immunities clause meant there were two separate types of citizenship—federal and state—and that federal citizenship took precedence, given that the Constitution is "the supreme law of the land." Since black Americans were federal citizens—part of "We the People"—state laws to the contrary were null and void. It also meant slavery was unconstitutional, since it inevitably deprived black Americans of their federally guaranteed privileges and immunities.

True, the Constitution included provisions that obliquely protected slavery, including one that required the return of runaways and another that counted each slave as three-fifths of a person when allocating Congressional representatives. But even these provisions had innocent explanations, according to the antislavery theorists. The so-called fugitive slave clause—which actually uses the term "person[s] held to service," not "slaves"—really applied to indentured servants and runaway apprentices, they said, and while the three-fifths clause recognized the existence of slavery, they pointed out that it gave slavery no legal protection. On the contrary, it rewarded states with more congressional representation if they freed their slaves. Not a word of the Constitution would have to be changed, Douglass observed, for Congress to eradicate slavery nationwide.

White southerners took the opposite position: not only was slavery constitutionally guaranteed, in their view, but there was no such thing as federal citizenship at all. Citizenship was solely a state matter. That, in turn, implied that states could even secede from the union, since, if there were no federal citizens, then the federal government could not be sovereign. Only the states were sovereign, and the federal Constitution was really just a treaty between them, akin to a league of independent nations.

This argument ignored the fact that the Constitution had been written for the very purpose of eliminating the treaty-style system that prevailed under the Articles of Confederation,[12] and that the Constitution explicitly refers to federal citizenship, while using only the word "inhabitant"—not citizen—when referring to state residency. The Constitution also gives Congress power to pass naturalization laws, which would make no sense unless federal citizenship was separate from, and superior to, state law.

These disputes over the constitutional status of slavery, which began in earnest in the 1830s, reached their climax in 1857 when

Chief Justice Taney announced his ruling in the *Dred Scott* case: black Americans, even if they were not slaves, could never be citizens.[13] Two years later, the State Department denied Douglass a passport on the grounds that he was not a citizen.[14] Not until the Fourteenth Amendment was ratified in 1868 did the Constitution define federal citizenship and expressly protect federal rights against state interference. That achievement came about only through the leadership of anti-slavery constitutionalists like Smith and Douglass, who, when the Civil War ended, seized the brief window of opportunity to amend the Constitution in a way that ensured their understanding of the document would be forever enshrined in the nation's highest law.

While Douglass was studying these constitutional arguments in the 1850s, he was also coming to reject Garrison's pacifism. Alongside his own experience, particularly his fight with Covey, Douglass was inspired by the story of the rebellion a decade earlier aboard the slave ship *Creole*, led by a Virginian slave aptly named Madison Washington. Less well known than the *Amistad* uprising, the *Creole* mutiny struck Douglass as a real-life adventure of the liberty struggle. He was not the only one; it inspired Herman Melville's story *Benito Cereno* in 1855. But in 1852, Douglass published his own novella based on it, entitled *The Heroic Slave*, regarded as one of the first works of fiction ever published by a black American author. Another inspiration was the 1851 "Jerry Rescue," in which a group of abolitionists led by Gerrit Smith helped a fugitive slave named William "Jerry" McHenry escape to freedom. Smith, Douglass gushed, had raised abolitionism to "the Jerry level."[15]

But more even than these, what inspired Douglass's thinking on the future of anti-slavery work was his meeting in 1847 with the militant abolitionist John Brown. A friend of Smith's, Brown was living in North Elba, New York, about 300 miles northeast of Rochester, on land Smith had sold him. Brown was a shepherd, a failed businessman, and a religious fanatic who pledged his life to the destruction of slavery when, as a boy of 12, he witnessed a white man beating a slave with an iron shovel. Like Douglass, he had started out as a Garrisonian pacifist, but came to reject that view and to embrace the idea that violence in a righteous cause could serve the Lord's will. He must have been a man of intense charisma, for notwithstanding his Puritanical attitudes and Spartan habits, he inspired absolute devotion even in people who thought his religious beliefs silly. Douglass, anything but an Old Testament Christian, was nevertheless entranced. To the end of his life, he considered Brown among the "greatest heroes known to American fame."[16]

Brown consulted with Douglass on a plan he was drafting to raise a guerilla army that, using the Allegeny Mountains as a base, would infiltrate the South, harass slaveholders, and encourage uprisings. Although he found the idea intriguing, Douglass concluded that the plan was doomed. Still, he was beginning to believe that something like it was necessary. "I continued to write and speak against slavery," he wrote later, but "all the same" he had become "less hopeful of its peaceful abolition."[17] Brown chose not to proceed with this hazily formulated scheme and moved west instead, where he participated in the undeclared war between pro- and anti-slavery forces that would later be called "Bleeding Kansas."

The chasm between the Garrisonian anarchist version of abolitionism and Gerrit Smith's theory of political engagement and constitutionalism reveals a pattern common to reform movements even today. On the one hand, radicals resist engaging in a political system that they view as irretrievably tainted. To participate, even by voting, is to lend credibility to that system, and to settle for half-measures, as the political world often requires, means to surrender the demand for justice. On the other hand, prioritizing moral purity at the expense of political participation often means passing up opportunities for real, if piecemeal, reform—making the best the enemy of the good. Douglass came to conclude that the Garrisonian position of nonengagement—refusing to vote, run for office, or support violent rebellion—only meant postponing the real work of freeing the slaves. If abolitionists persisted in that vein, they would be "scattered and left to wander, and to die in the wilderness, like God's ancient people, till another generation shall come up, more worthy to go up and possess the land."[18]

These political differences were sharpened, however, by a personal clash that permanently severed Garrison's relationship with Douglass. The incident involved Julia Griffiths, the Englishwoman Douglass had met during his British tour in 1846, and who had come to Rochester to help edit *Frederick Douglass' Paper*. For a time, she lived in the family's home. But in 1853, *The Liberator* published a scandalous report that Douglass's wife Anna had banished her from the house after some sort of fight. Another paper labeled Griffiths "a Jezebel" who was "making mischief" in the family.[19] Douglass responded by sending *The Liberator* a letter, over his wife's name, insisting that nothing untoward had happened. Today, the exact nature of Douglass's relationship with Griffiths remains unclear, but it is at least true that Griffiths did move out of the house, likely as a result of Anna's complaints, and that Douglass maintained a flirtatious tone in his correspondence with her and with several other women.

It is not hard to imagine a romance between him and Griffiths. The marriage between Frederick and Anna Douglass has long been a mystery to biographers, as he virtually never mentioned her in his writings. In a memoir published in 1900, their daughter Rosetta described her mother as strict, often stern, with a vein of sarcastic humor, but otherwise a no-nonsense housewife who took pride in a well-run home. She was not a crusader like her husband. Most remarkably, she remained illiterate her entire life, notwithstanding the immense value Douglass placed on reading and writing and the fact that, according to Rosetta, she "greatly deplored" her illiteracy.[20] Given these clues, it is easy to picture

Douglas being attracted to the articulate and passionate women who participated in the cause to which he devoted himself. Whatever the facts may be, Griffiths continued to work with Douglass until 1855, when she returned home to England, and they continued to correspond for the rest of her life.[21]

# 6. The War: 1852–1865

Sociologist Orlando Patterson argues that the history of individual liberty begins with slaves, who "first came to value its absence,"[1] but that "[n]ot until the master had good reason to conspire with the slave's brute instinct to be free" could the slave's yearning for freedom be recognized as a social value.[2] Frederick Douglass's experiences in the 1850s parallel the history of freedom as Patterson imagines it. The decade before the Civil War saw the censorship of anti-slavery publications, the savage beating of abolitionist Sen. Charles Sumner, the bloody clashes between pro- and anti-slavery militia in Kansas, and the cruel and intrusive mandates of the Fugitive Slave Act. All these and more gave northerners increasing reason to "conspire" with the longing for freedom so eloquently expressed by escaped slaves like Douglass. White Americans came to realize that the choice was between the perpetuation of slavery or the survival of the Constitution and the nation.

The path of that discovery was suggested by a speech Douglass delivered in Rochester on July 5, 1852, entitled "What to the Slave Is the Fourth of July?" Douglass expressed in magnificent rhetoric the depths of misery that enslaved people faced, his resentment toward the land that tolerated and even encouraged their subjugation, and his rapturous discovery that the nation's highest law was, in actuality, an anti-slavery charter. "Interpreted as it ought to be interpreted," he declared, "the Constitution is a GLORIOUS LIBERTY DOCUMENT."[3]

Douglass emphasized the long-standing rule that the Constitution must be interpreted whenever possible to favor freedom, not slavery—even when such an interpretation might seem like a stretch. "Where rights are infringed," wrote the venerated Chief Justice John Marshall in an 1805 case, "the legislative intention must be expressed with irresistible clearness, to induce a court of justice to suppose a design to effect such objects."[4] But the words "slavery," "slaveholding," and "slave" do not appear in the Constitution. Thus, said Douglass, people who claimed that slavery was constitutionally protected were in the position of a man who claimed to hold a deed to land "in which no mention of land was made." Douglass believed it was the pro-slavery lawyers, who claimed that the Constitution protected an institution it did not even refer to by name, who were indulging in strained interpretations. Ordinary Americans who heeded them were allowing themselves to be "ruinously imposed upon." Although many legal scholars today reject this argument, it is at least as plausible as the theory Chief Justice Taney would endorse in *Dred Scott* three years later. Yet, the myth that slavery was guaranteed by the Constitution was being spread not only by champions of slavery such as Taney, but also by the followers of William Lloyd Garrison. Douglass rejected both views. The Constitution's "principles and purposes," he insisted, were "entirely hostile to the existence of slavery,"[5] and Americans should embrace the nation's highest law as a charter of freedom.

As James Colaiaco writes in his book-length study of the "Fourth of July" oration, Douglass had by this time "become one of the foremost advocates for the United States Constitution."[6] And the speech became one of his finest achievements. Yet, his audience must have found it hard to envision the glowing future of liberty evoked by his words. The 1850s brought the fortunes of abolitionists to their lowest ebb. Shortly before Douglass spoke, Congress enacted a group of laws collectively called the Compromise of 1850. The new legislation transformed the political landscape by overturning the 30-year-old Missouri Compromise whereby Congress had promised to confine slavery to the southeast.

Under the new arrangement, voters in what is now Utah, Nevada, New Mexico, and Arizona could decide without federal interference whether or not to implement slavery. The deal also included a powerful new Fugitive Slave Act, which expanded slave owners' power to reclaim runaways. In exchange for these concessions, slavery's opponents got the admission of California as a free state and the abolition of the slave trade—but not slavery—in Washington, D.C. The compromise was thus a massive win for the slave power, but moderates once again swallowed their objections in hopes that this would finally end decades of tension between North and South.

It took only four years for that hope to unravel. In 1854, Congress passed the Kansas-Nebraska Act, which allowed the people in those territories, too, to choose slavery if they wished, thus erasing the last limits imposed by the Missouri Compromise. Resistance to the Fugitive Slave Act began to intensify in northern states, partly because the act forced civilians to aid in the recapture of runaways, and partly because of a provision that paid judges more for ruling against alleged escapees than for ruling in their favor. In June of that year, President Franklin Pierce, determined to demonstrate the federal government's resolve to enforce the act, dispatched 2,000 soldiers to Boston to recapture a single fugitive. That outrageous show of force only drove more moderates into the anti-slavery camp. "We went to bed one night old-fashioned, conservative[s]," wrote one Bostonian, "and waked up stark mad abolitionists."[7]

Three years later, the deal changed once more, when the Supreme Court ruled in *Dred Scott* that Congress could not ban slavery in the federal territories at all. "[T]he right of property in a slave is distinctly and expressly affirmed in the Constitution," Chief Justice Taney asserted. Congress thus had no authority to forbid it in the West. "The only power conferred is the power coupled with the duty of guarding and protecting the owner in his rights."[8] By that reasoning, slavery was not only sacrosanct on the frontier, but it was also protected by federal law throughout the states. If slavery was "distinctly and expressly affirmed" in the Constitution, then state laws against slavery, no less than territorial prohibitions, would inevitably clash with "the supreme law of the land." If that weren't already clear from the *Dred Scott* ruling, it would only take a follow-up decision to make it so.

Two months after the decision was announced, Douglass condemned it in a rousing oration before an audience in New York. It was a "hell-black judgment" that "cannot stand." In fact, it was in some sense a blessing to the anti-slavery cause—a "necessary link in the chain of events preparatory to the downfall and complete overthrow of the slave system."[9] The decision was so poorly reasoned, he insisted, it could not stand the test of public debate; if anything, it made clear to the nation that the freedom of white and black Americans was necessarily intertwined.

But while Douglass was confident that the opinion would spell the death of slavery in the long run, advocates of freedom would have to rethink their approach if they were to succeed. Garrison's motto, "no union with slaveholders," was exactly backward. In fact, Douglass thought it morally reprehensible, because it prioritized the ethical purity of white abolitionists over the actual work of liberating captives. In their insistence that the Constitution was evil because it was a pro-slavery document, the Garrisonians were essentially aligned with the *Dred Scott* decision: the notion that the Constitution's authors meant to protect slavery was "Judge Taney's argument, and it is Mr. Garrison's argument, but it is not the argument of the Constitution."[10] It was time to put away that error and to rally around the Constitution—to use it to secure the blessings of liberty for all Americans.

That meant abandoning the pacifist, nonpolitical doctrines that left slaves with nobody to speak for them in the political arena. "If I were on board of a pirate ship, with a company of men and women whose lives and liberties I had put in jeopardy," Douglass insisted, "I would not clear my soul of their blood by jumping in the long boat, and singing out no union with pirates."[11] Not only did the nation's highest law provide no permanent security for slavery, it actually prohibited slavery by guaranteeing due process, forbidding bills of attainder, and promising that all people would be secure and free.[12] "All I ask of the American people is that they live up to the Constitution, adopt its principles, imbibe its spirit, and enforce its provisions."[13]

By this time, Douglass had thoroughly revised his *Narrative*, lengthening it by several chapters. He published it in 1855, under the more dramatic title *My Bondage and My Freedom*, with a dedication to Garrison's nemesis, Gerrit Smith. The book sounded a more rebellious note than the previous version; it condemned the pro-slavery churches more vocally, justified the right of slaves to steal from their masters, and even celebrated the notion of killing slave catchers. It ended with a chapter reflecting on Douglass's break with the Garrisonians: he regretted that they "could not see any honest reasons" for his change of mind about the Constitution—and, he claimed, they were "not entirely recovered" from the racism that infected American society.[14]

Garrison was outraged. But he, in turn, could snicker at how little progress Smith and Douglass were making in their political efforts. Not only was Smith's Liberty Party ineffective, but its efforts to gain influence were leading its members into just the sort of moral compromises that Garrison warned about. The worst had come in 1848, when the party—which had merged with allied groups to form the new Free Soil Party—chose Martin Van Buren as its presidential nominee. Van Buren was an unprincipled schemer who not only lacked anti-slavery credentials, but, as president a decade earlier, had overseen the expulsion of the Cherokee from their Georgia lands and tried unsuccessfully to reenslave the *Amistad* rebels. Yet, the political abolitionists overlooked these flaws in hopes that his name recognition would help their ticket. That did not happen. The Free Soil Party disappeared, eventually morphing into the Republican Party.

The Garrisonians thought the fiasco vindicated their belief that political abolitionism was futile, even counterproductive, because politics required compromises that would lend moral credence to a corrupt system. Douglass, however, saw compromise as an inevitable price of actually getting reforms accomplished. "It is easy to say that this or that measure would have been wiser or better," he wrote. But "the experience of reform in all ages" is that engaged people do what they can to reach political goals—and halfway measures must sometimes be accepted as better than nothing.[15] The nonpolitical alternative offered by the Garrisonians was unacceptable; indeed, it was "an abandonment of the great idea" of the abolitionist movement, which had started out intending to free the slave, but by repudiating political involvement "ends by leaving the slave to free himself."[16]

Douglass, of course, also believed in slaves freeing themselves. In February 1858, John Brown again appeared at Douglass's Rochester home. He stayed for weeks, writing to friends to ask for money and fashioning an elaborate scheme to create a system of forts in the Allegheny Mountains that would serve as headquarters for a guerilla war against the slave states. Douglass admired Brown's commitment, and his youngest child, Annie, came to adore Brown, who delighted her with stories. Douglass eventually grew bored with Brown's monomania and his obsessive explanations of his plans, and Brown departed for some secretive meetings with supporters in Boston, after which he decided to return to Kansas, rather than pursue his guerilla scheme. He returned a year later, once more visiting Douglass briefly before hustling off for more clandestine conferences. Finally, in August 1859, Douglass got a message from Brown summoning him to a rendezvous at a stone quarry in Pennsylvania. There, Brown disclosed his plans for a military assault on the federal armory in Harper's Ferry, in what was then Virginia. He asked Douglass to join him.

Douglass thought the plan was suicidal and refused. Over the next few weeks, Brown sent him more messages, urging him to change his mind; but when Douglass still said no, he went through with the plot himself. On October 16, he led a group of 22 amateur soldiers to attack the arsenal. They almost captured the town but were swiftly trapped in the stockade. After a brief standoff, the insurrectionists were overcome. Brown was arrested and charged with treason.

It was a precarious position for Douglass. His many meetings with Brown, and the correspondence between the two, were certain to be discovered by federal prosecutors; and although he had chosen not to participate in the attack, he had raised money for Brown and had praised him in his newspaper. One of the insurrectionists had joined Brown only after accompanying Douglass to the quarry meeting. These facts alone would probably suffice to convict Douglass of conspiracy.

Douglass was on stage in Philadelphia giving his "Self-Made Men" lecture when an arrest warrant arrived. Fortunately, the telegraph operator was a fellow abolitionist, and he held off delivering the message long enough to give Douglass time to flee.[17] He left immediately for Rochester, where he packed and crossed into Canada and from there took a steamer to England in November. His worst fears seemed realized when the *New York Herald* announced that, under interrogation, Brown had "made a full statement, implicating Gerrit Smith, [anti-slavery Rep.] Joshua Giddings, and Frederick Douglass."[18] In fact, Brown had taken full responsibility himself; but it is almost certain that, if Douglass had stayed, he would have been arrested and subjected to a show trial to vindicate Virginia's interests in the "peculiar institution." That December, the state hanged Brown for treason.

Five months later, Douglass was in Scotland when he received the devastating news that his youngest child, Annie, had died. At only 12 years old, she was her father's darling. Just months before, she had sent him a plaintive letter, bemoaning the death of her friend John Brown. "They took him in an open field and about a half a mile from the jail and hung him," she wrote.[19] Brown's death and her father's absence seem to have hastened her own death from an unknown illness.[20] Disregarding the risk of arrest, he rushed back to the United States, arriving in May 1860, long after her funeral. Douglass's heartache over her loss was severe enough to worry his family. His letter home in response to the bad news no longer exists, but his eldest daughter, Rosetta, told a friend that it indicated he had lost his "composure of mind."[21] He never ceased to grieve.

Douglass was not arrested upon his return, and he was always puzzled by "the sudden abandonment" of the congressional investigation into the Harper's Ferry incident.[22] The simple explanation was that the country's attention had turned by that time to the accelerating crisis between the states. Within weeks of Douglass's homecoming, the Republican Party surprised the nation by nominating for the presidency the relative newcomer, former Rep. Abraham Lincoln. This time it was slavery's defenders who were unable to agree on a candidate. With Democrats divided into northern and southern factions, Lincoln won in November, despite his name not even appearing on southern ballots. Within weeks, the Deep South began moving toward secession.

Douglass was not initially an admirer of Lincoln. His choice for president was Gerrit Smith. His second choice would likely have been William Seward, the abolitionist and former New York governor who had been the leading Republican candidate before the convention. "The Republican Party is justly proud of Mr. Seward," Douglass wrote. "[I]t is not without strong feeling that it sees him shoved aside to make room for a man whose abilities are untried, and whose political history is too meagre to form a basis on which to judge of his future."[23]

But not only was Lincoln untried, he was far too equivocal for Douglass's tastes. Lincoln considered slavery a moral crime, and affirmed that people of all races were entitled to equal rights. Yet he temporized for years, and during the war his maddening patience made it impossible for Douglass to come to a simple verdict on the Great Emancipator's place in history. He admired the president's eloquence and political skills, and respected his ability to hold firm when necessary, but he could never forget that Lincoln always approached slavery and the war primarily in terms of how they affected white Americans, rather than how they affected the Americans in bondage.[24]

Many abolitionists greeted the outbreak of war the following spring with joy—immediately recognizing that it meant the beginning of the end for slavery. The attack on Fort Sumter completed the process of giving white America a reason to conspire with the slave's longing for freedom. "God be praised! That it has come at last," exulted Douglass.[25] But the president, from both conviction and circumstance, insisted that his goal in putting down the rebellion was only to keep the union intact; he barely hinted at the possibility of ending slavery, even after Union troops suffered routs at Bull Run and Ball's Bluff.

In February 1862, Douglass told listeners at the Tremont Temple in Boston, "[T]he most painful and mortifying feature presented in the prosecution and management of the present war" was not that Confederate forces were proving more formidable than predicted; it was "the vacillation, doubt, uncertainty and hesitation, which have thus far distinguished our government in regard to the true method of dealing with the vital cause of the rebellion."[26] Freeing the slaves was a moral and military necessity, yet the president seemed unwilling to see it.

As the war ground on, Douglass fumed that the administration seemed intent on doing *"evil by choice, right from necessity."*[27] Even a decade after the war, he considered Lincoln "preeminently the white man's president,"[28] who had taken a noble course, but only in baby steps and only when events deprived him of other options. That did not mean Lincoln was not great, he continued, because the president's honesty and "heroic spirit" led him to meet the challenges of his time boldly and to vindicate principle when the crisis came.[29] Yet Lincoln could not be viewed as a wholehearted benefactor to the black man.

In fact, as late as the end of 1862 Lincoln was still considering, apparently with all seriousness, the possibility of colonizing freed slaves to Africa. He told a delegation of black leaders in an August meeting that they should take advantage of a congressional proposal to establish a colony there and, in December, proposed in his annual message to Congress that the Constitution be amended to provide for colonization. This was anathema to Douglass but not to all black leaders. Toward the end of the war, Lincoln even met warmly with Martin Delany, who had once been Douglass's coeditor on *The North Star* before the two split over Delany's support for colonization. Lincoln appointed Delany a major in the Army, and although he promised Douglass a similar appointment, that never came about. Douglass was infuriated by the talk of colonization—"ten thousand times refuted," in his view. "What shall be done with the four million slaves if they are emancipated?" he wrote.

> Our answer is, do nothing with them; mind your business, and let them mind theirs. Your *doing* with them is their greatest misfortune. They have been undone by your doings, and all they now ask, and really have need of at your hands, is just to let them alone. . . . As colored men, we only ask to be allowed to *do* with ourselves. . . . Let us stand upon our own legs, work with our own hands, and eat bread in the sweat of our own brows.[30]

The Administration's talk of colonization petered out at the beginning of 1863, when Lincoln followed through on his promise to proclaim the slaves in the rebel states "forever free." The Emancipation Proclamation was a military order, aimed at sapping enemy manpower and ending the previous policy of returning runaways to masters. It did not free slaves in the border states, although it did protect them from being sold south. In any case, abolitionists cheered when it was pronounced final on January 1, 1863. They had half expected Lincoln to back down, just as he had nixed previous efforts to free slaves, most notably Gen. John C. Frémont's order liberating the human property of Confederate supporters in Missouri two years before. Fearful that the order would drive Missouri out of the union, Lincoln had overruled it. So, when abolitionists gathered in Boston on New Year's Day to await the announcement that the final proclamation had been issued, there was much trepidation.

"Eight, nine, ten o'clock came and went," as Douglass recalled. Finally, when "suspense was becoming agony," the message arrived, and crowds at Tremont Temple and Boston Music Hall burst into celebration.[31] Douglass led the crowd at the Temple in a chorus of his favorite hymn, "Blow, Ye Trumpet, Blow" ("Ye slaves of sin and hell,/your liberty receive. . . . The year of jubilee is come!"). After the Emancipation Proclamation, Douglass claimed, exultant abolitionists were "willing to allow the President all the latitude of time, phraseology, and every honorable device that statesmanship might require for the achievement of a great and beneficent measure of liberty and progress."[32] That was an exaggeration—Lincoln's patience outpaced Douglass's time and again—but Douglass nevertheless saw the Emancipation Proclamation, whatever its limits, as a heroic deed.

The proclamation hinted that freed slaves might be allowed to join the Union army, and that issue brought Douglass to meet Lincoln in the White House on August 10, 1863. He found the president friendly, respectful, and relaxed, almost like an older brother. He was most impressed when Lincoln asked the governor of Connecticut, who had come for a meeting, to wait so his conversation with Douglass could continue. "This was probably the first time in the history of this Republic when its chief magistrate had found an occasion or shown a disposition to exercise such an act of impartiality," Douglass wrote in the 1880s.[33]

By then, Lincoln was a martyr and a symbol of a great cause, and Douglass was inclined to overlook their differences. But during the meeting itself, those differences were plain. The military was paying black soldiers less than whites, and Douglass was firm: all soldiers deserved the same, regardless of race. The president politely said no. Enlisting them at all was radical enough; to equalize their pay before whites were ready for that would harm morale.

Douglass moved on to his second point: the army should make clear that it would retaliate for any mistreatment of prisoners of war by the Confederates. On this, too, Lincoln demurred. Douglass was civil with the president, but not satisfied. Afterward, he was harsh: "The most malignant Copperhead in the country cannot reproach him with any undue solicitude for the lives and liberties of the brave black men who are now giving their arms and hearts to the support of this Government," he wrote.[34] But Douglass may have underestimated his own influence on Lincoln. Not only was it extraordinary by the standards of that day for the president to consult professionally with a black man at all, but Lincoln eventually did adopt both equal pay and retaliation for the mistreatment of black troops.

By that time, Douglass was employing all of his writing and speaking skills to recruit soldiers for the all-black 54th Massachusetts Regiment. Even his sons Lewis and Charles joined. On July 18, 1863, the regiment gained immortal fame by its bold attack on Fort Wagner, South Carolina, which ended with 272 casualties out of a total force of 600. Charles was ill and not at the battle; but Lewis was wounded, and a resulting sickness eventually forced him out of the army. The regiment's valor proved the mettle of black soldiers and, Douglass believed, demonstrated the worthiness of former slaves for the full rights and responsibilities of citizenship.

These two things were never separate in his mind. Black Americans, he believed, deserved not just freedom from slavery, but the deeper respect that comes from recognition of shared civic responsibility. Citizenship meant not merely freedom of speech, but the obligation to speak—not merely liberty, but the duty to defend that liberty, both with arms and with the vote. Freedom, he was fond of saying, depended on three boxes: "the ballot-box, the jury-box, and the cartridge-box."[35] The bravery of black soldiers showed that they were the equal of all Union men—and better than the white traitors of the South. Handed guns, they proved themselves worthy. If allowed to vote, they would prove worthy of that, as well.

Douglass next met with Lincoln during the war's dark days, in the late summer of 1864. The fighting had gone so badly for the North by that time that Lincoln feared the coming election would end his presidency and that the Democratic candidate, Gen. George McClellan, would make terms that would effectively surrender the cause. On August 23, he asked the members of his cabinet to sign a paper without reading it, in order to witness its date. On this so-called Blind Memorandum, the gloomy president had written that it was "exceedingly probable that this Administration will not be re-elected," and that if it was not, he would try "to co-operate with the president elect, as to save the Union between the election and the inauguration; as he will have secured his election on such ground that he can not possibly save it afterwards."[36]

Such foreboding was reasonable enough. Gen. William Sherman's forces were stalled outside Atlanta, and the public was showing signs of impatience. Only two weeks before he wrote the Blind Memorandum, Lincoln met with Douglass a second time to discuss a plan to smuggle slaves to freedom if the election went to his opponent—a scheme Douglass described as "somewhat after the original plan of John Brown."[37] The idea seems to have been for small squads of black soldiers to make their way from plantation to plantation liberating and arming slaves. Douglass was impressed. The president's words "showed a deeper moral conviction against slavery than I had ever seen before in anything spoken or written by him."[38] But in early September, Sherman broke through and took Atlanta, and the plan was rendered unnecessary. Lincoln was reelected and the South's fate was sealed.

Douglass was on hand for the inauguration festivities on March 4, 1865, and was once again awed by the president's civility. When policemen tried to throw him out of the reception, Lincoln interceded. "Here comes my friend Douglass," he announced loudly, holding out his hand. "I saw you in the crowd today, listening to my inaugural address; how did you like it?" He seemed genuinely pleased when Douglass answered that it was "a sacred effort."[39]

Weeks later, Union forces captured the Confederate capital, Richmond, and Lincoln decided to visit the city himself. When he stepped ashore from a boat rowed by military aides, a crowd of freedmen immediately recognized him. One fell to his knees. An embarrassed Lincoln lifted him to his feet. "That is not right," he said. "You must kneel to God only, and thank him for the liberty you will hereafter enjoy."[40] Soon afterward, Confederate Gen. Robert E. Lee surrendered his forces, and the war was effectively over.

Back in Washington, Lincoln sketched plans for the reconstruction of the South. He told a White House gathering on April 10 that the nation could now feel "hope of a righteous and speedy peace,"[41] but he once again sounded a moderate note about the terms he would impose on readmitting Confederate states to the union. He endorsed a proposal by Louisiana to return to the fold with laws that banned slavery but did not grant full voting rights to freedmen. "It is unsatisfactory to some that the elective franchise is not given to the colored man," he acknowledged. Yet, he offered a deferential alternative. "I would myself prefer that it were now conferred on the very intelligent, and on those who serve our cause as soldiers. Still the question is not whether the

Louisiana government, as it stands, is quite all that is desirable. The question is 'Will it be wiser to take it as it is, and help to improve it; or to reject, and disperse it?'"[42] We will never know whether Douglass would have castigated the Great Emancipator for such appeasement, because four nights later, Lincoln fell to the assassin's bullet.

Historians debate how much influence Douglass had on Lincoln, and Douglass himself was never sure. He struggled, even after the president was martyred, to form a final judgment of Lincoln's policies. During the war, he found it hard to understand why Lincoln was so slow to lead his fellow whites to implement principles that were so clearly just and so plainly practical as emancipation, equal pay, and voting rights. For his part, Lincoln seems to have embraced those principles but agonized over prudent ways to implement them, given how many of his allies wanted no part in a fight for abolition. At times, that dilemma pushed Lincoln into what looked like betrayal. But he gradually moved in Douglass's direction, partly because of the inexorable logic of events—that is, the clash of ideas behind the war that made slavery's death inevitable—or, as Douglass put it, "the mighty current of eternal principles—invisible forces, which are shaping and fashioning events as they wish."[43]

When Lincoln's widow made a gift to Douglass of the late president's walking stick, he thanked her by saying he would treasure the "inestimable memento" as a token of "his humane interest in the welfare of my whole race."[44] Yet, he could never forget, as he later said, that Lincoln had "shared the prejudices of his white fellow-countrymen against the Negro."[45] In the end, the president disappointed Douglass because he was a president, not a prophet. He had been diligent in his duty, rather than proclaiming a new covenant. At war's end, justice had triumphed but had not been vindicated. Vindication, as Lincoln recognized, might very well have required that "every drop of blood drawn with the lash shall be paid by another drawn with the sword."[46]

# 7. Reconstruction: 1865–1876

Lincoln's murder was a catastrophe for those who, like Douglass, thought "the mission of this war is National regeneration."[1] It put the alcoholic racist Andrew Johnson in the White House, where for the next four years he went to great effort to obstruct the work of civil rights. Douglass had observed Johnson drunk at Lincoln's second inauguration and remarked that he was "no friend of our race."[2] But it was worse than that: the Tennessean had been placed on the ticket for vice president only to emphasize that the administration's cause was focused on defending the Union, rather than freeing the slaves. Now, with representatives of southern states waiting to be readmitted to Congress, the anti-slavery Republicans had the opportunity to demand protections for the freedmen as the price of reconciliation. But when they passed the Civil Rights Act of 1866, Johnson vetoed it.

Republicans overrode that veto and drafted the Fourteenth Amendment, which, when it was ratified in July 1868, finally defined citizenship and guaranteed basic rights against violation by state governments. But for the rest of his term, Johnson pursued an extraordinary program of obstruction that extinguished many of the opportunities created by Union victory. As historian Douglas Egerton writes, Johnson "signaled to his fellow white southerners that he would demand almost nothing of them"; and although northerners did at first make demands, they mostly ceased trying by the end of the century.[3] By then, many of the gains of the Reconstruction era had been snatched back by revanchist Confederates.

For his part, Douglass was clear from the moment the guns ceased firing that the work of rededicating American society to the principle of equal freedom had just begun. Weeks after Lincoln's death, he spoke at a meeting of the American Anti-Slavery Society to oppose Garrison's motion to shutter the organization on the grounds that its mission was accomplished. "Slavery is not abolished until the black man has the ballot," Douglass insisted— or so long as southern states kept black Americans from owning firearms for self-defense or maintained segregated schools and railcars.[4] Douglass prevailed, and the society turned its attention to Reconstruction. Garrison chose to retire.

In February 1866, Douglass led a delegation to meet with President Johnson to ask directly that the government do more to guarantee the rights of freedmen, particularly the right to vote. Johnson took it badly. It was offensive, he told Douglass, to be "arraigned by some one who can get up handsomely rounded periods and deal in rhetoric and talk about abstract ideas of liberty, who never periled life, liberty, or property." At one point he demanded of Douglass, "Have you ever lived upon a plantation?" When Douglass said he had, Johnson launched into a diatribe in which he blamed the war on the wealthy minority of southern slaveowners and insisted that now that they had been defeated, political power should be inherited by the poor whites who had been "forced into the rebellion." Enfranchising former slaves over white objections would be "tyranny," he thought. "It is a fundamental tenet in my creed that the people must be obeyed. Is there anything wrong or unfair in that?"

With a smile, Douglass could only answer, "A great deal wrong, Mr. President, with all respect."[5] Johnson seemed not to hear and rambled awkwardly for a few more minutes, before concluding that the freedmen should just leave the country and establish colonies elsewhere. Douglass answered politely, though after the delegates left, the President growled to his secretary, "I know that damned Douglass; he's just like any nigger."[6] Later that day,

Douglass wrote a letter to the editor of the *Washington Chronicle* to protest: "the worst enemy of the nation could not cast upon its fair name a greater infamy than to suppose that Negroes could be tolerated among them in a state of the most degrading slavery and oppression, and must be cast away, driven into exile, for no other cause than having been freed from their chains."[7] When word reached Douglass that Johnson was considering offering him leadership of the Freedmen's Bureau, he declined, recognizing that to be beholden to the president would ruin his reputation and destroy his self-esteem.

Douglass also maintained his independence from congressional Republicans. He never joined in efforts by some leaders, including Charles Sumner, to confiscate plantation land and divide it among the former slaves.[8] One Douglass scholar has detected in this a "bourgeois" commitment to property rights that "confounded his conception of Reconstruction, thereby undermining its viability."[9] But it is more likely that Douglass was too well versed in the history and theory of freedom not to know that destabilizing property rights in such a way would in the long run harm the freedmen more. What they needed was more liberty to earn a living and keep the fruits of their labor, not paternalism, control, and oversight by a government dominated by whites. Although government could legitimately provide the freedmen with less intrusive forms of aid, the power to redistribute land, however well intentioned, was dangerous: it could easily fall into the hands of the politically powerful—which meant racist whites—who would then exploit that power for their own benefit.[10]

Interference with justly acquired property contradicted the basic principle of Douglass's political beliefs. To take away a worker's earnings, he believed, "was the right of the robber."[11] It would also be robbery to take away inherited property—after all, the most basic property right of all is one's body, which one does not earn, but inherits. Either way, self-reliance and dignity required respect for property rights. "No man has a right to live unless he lives honestly," he told an audience in 1877, "and no man lives honestly who lives upon another."[12] Thus, he was unsympathetic to the newfangled theories of socialism and communism, which he saw as based on a false equivalence between the ownership of property and of people. In 1848, he had upbraided a communist speaker who told an anti-slavery meeting that the ownership of land was as evil as the ownership of human beings. He was astonished that "anyone could listen with patience to such arrant nonsense." The ownership of soil was "no harm. . . . It is right that [people] should own it." But slavery was a "sin against self-evident truth."[13]

Although Douglass rarely addressed socialism explicitly, further light is thrown on his views by the words of his first biographer, Frederic May Holland, whose 1891 book was prepared with Douglass's active involvement. "The present views of Mr. Douglass," Holland wrote, were that while "our existing system of free labor in keen competition has many defects," it had "succeeded much better than any other, not only in increasing the general wealth, to the benefit of even the poorest, but in developing individual energy, intelligence, industry, economy, foresight, perseverance, and self-control." Socialism had failed even in religious communities such as the Puritans, and in those communities where it seemed to succeed, it did so only on account of "the willingness of the members to live very cheaply" and to "yield the most submissive obedience to superiors who keep them at work." People would only produce for two reasons: private profit or compulsion. And if an entire nation tried the socialist experiment, "very severe punishments would have to be employed" to keep people working. Thus "any general system of compulsory labor would necessarily resemble slavery, in all its cruelties as well as its privations. The only alternative, besides our competitive system, is one which has too much in common with negro slavery." Capitalism was simply "the only system of labor which a lover of liberty can favor consistently."[14]

Douglass's thinking may also have been influenced by the dolorous condition of the Native Americans, and of the Irish in Great Britain, whose social and geographical isolation had made them easier targets of oppression and extermination. He frequently emphasized that the "only thing that has saved the Negro" from a fate similar to that of Native Americans was "his being brought into the American body politic."[15] Policies premised on separatism and on regarding black Americans as dependents who must be "given" land—anything, in short, other than integration into the people of the United States—would ultimately lead to the same ills that federal Indian policy had inflicted. To become an object of official pity and be treated as a separate caste was, he feared, a recipe for permanent racial subordination or even genocide.

In short, government reallocation of property was to Douglass just another example of the futile effort to "give" freedom to black Americans—something he consistently denounced. He thought the freedmen should aim at self-reliance—which he considered both a duty and a right. He had emphasized his "leave us alone" approach shortly before the war ended when he told an audience that

> in regard to the colored people, there is always more that is benevolent, I perceive, than just, manifested towards us. What I ask for the negro is not benevolence, not pity, not sympathy, but simply *justice*. The American people have always been anxious to know what they shall do with us. . . . I have had but one answer from the beginning. Do nothing with us! Your doing with us has already played the mischief with us. Do nothing with us! If the apples will not remain on the tree of their own strength, if they are worm-eaten at the core, if they are early ripe and disposed to fall, let them fall! I am not for tying or fastening them on the tree in any way, except by nature's plan, and if they will not stay there, let them fall. And if the negro cannot stand on his own legs, let him fall also. All I ask is,

> give him a chance to stand on his own legs. . . ! If the negro
> cannot live by the line of eternal justice . . . the fault will
> not be yours, it will be his who made the negro. . . . Let
> him live or die by that. If you will only untie his hands,
> and give him a chance, I think he will live.[16]

This did not mean that Douglass viewed the plight of the freed-men unfeelingly or that he rejected in principle government efforts during Reconstruction to alleviate their suffering. On the contrary, he supported the work of the Freedmen's Bureau, established by Congress to protect blacks from violence and to promote their economic status by providing them with clothing, food, health care, and jobs. He even proposed a plan to use government funds to buy southern land and sell it in small lots to freedmen at discounted rates so that they "can then go to work and make themselves homes."[17] Clarifying his "leave us alone" views, he explained that he did "not solicit unusual favor but [only] rough-handed 'fair play.' We are neither lame nor blind, that we should seek to throw off the responsibility of our own existence, or to cast ourselves upon public charity."[18] But by "fair play" he meant "a good deal more than some understand. . . . It is not fair play to start the negro out in life, from nothing and with nothing. . . . Should the American people put a schoolhouse in every valley in the south and a church on every hillside," they "would not have given fair play."

There was no point in trying to compensate for the crimes of the past, but "the nearest approach to justice to the negro for the past is to do him justice in the present."[19] That meant integrating schools and ending legal barriers to employment and property ownership. Douglass recognized that there were limits to the good that government could accomplish. The real problem was "the American chimera called 'public opinion,'"[20] and that could be changed only by time, persuasion, and protest. Forcible redistribution and the creation of a government dependency system appeared to him dangerous and ultimately ineffective propositions. In the last analysis, Douglass saw racism as a social problem, not primarily a political one, and thus it had to be targeted primarily through social, not governmental means. "The settled habits of a nation," he said, "are mightier than a statute."[21]

In short, Douglass's political views are, with some exceptions,[22] best described as "classical liberal"—today often called "libertarian." That is why, like today's libertarians, he sometimes sounds conservative and sometimes liberal. Classical liberalism is committed to both personal and economic freedom and views all individual rights in terms of private property: a person's right to freedom is a manifestation of his rightful, inalienable ownership of his mind and body. His right to the fruits of his labor is deduced from the same principle.

Eric Foner, the foremost historian of the Reconstruction period, has argued that intellectuals in the decades surrounding the Civil War created a "Free Labor ideology" based on the dignity of labor and the social dynamism and moral justice that flows from each person's right to work at his calling.[23] But "Free Labor ideology" was not a 19th-century innovation. Douglass and his colleagues viewed it as a direct descendant of the classical liberalism of the American founding. Its basic principles are that all people are fundamentally free and equal—none the natural ruler over another—and, consequently, that each person has the right to pursue happiness without interference from others or from the state. Douglass was not, therefore, a conservative but a radical—a radical for individualism and for the "bourgeois virtues" of self-reliance, industry, and personal pride.[24] He was not likely to be attracted to any doctrine that subordinated individual rights—whether free speech or property rights—to the interests of the collective.

Douglass even viewed the right to vote—his primary focus in the decade after the war—primarily as a matter of self-defense, rather than as a tool for establishing new political institutions. The early years of Reconstruction saw astonishing advances in the social position of former slaves, with black candidates elected to state legislatures and even writing new state Constitutions. White terrorist groups such as the Ku Klux Klan struck back, and their supporters in government found legalistic ways to restrict black voting rights, particularly by imposing poll taxes, literacy tests, and the infamous grandfather clause whereby limits on voting were waived for men whose grandfathers had been allowed to vote. By effectively disenfranchising black voters, these tricks allowed white-dominated legislatures to impose an array of new deprivations on the freedmen—taking away their right to own firearms, for instance, or forcing them to satisfy expensive and time-consuming licensing requirements before getting jobs. In the same 1865 address in which Douglass demanded that whites "do nothing with us," he argued that voting rights were the "counterpoise" America needed against the insurgent "enmity" of southern whites. "Without the elective franchise, the Negro will still be practically a slave," he wrote to a friend. "Individual ownership has been abolished, but if we restore the Southern States without this measure, we shall establish an ownership of the blacks by the community among whom they live."[25]

Douglass thought that nothing short of a constitutional amendment guaranteeing voting rights for the freedmen could prevent that outcome. But here he ran into opposition from longstanding allies. When the Fourteenth Amendment was adopted in 1868, it included a provision that punished states if they denied suffrage "to any of the *male* inhabitants of such State." That was the first time this word had ever been placed in the Constitution, and advocates of female suffrage were outraged by the implication that states could constitutionally deny voting rights to their female inhabitants. Until then, they had argued—in an echo of Douglass's own anti-slavery constitutionalism—that women were citizens and nothing in the Constitution entitled states to interfere with their voting rights as Americans. In fact, women had voted in some states early in American history.[26] But the

Fourteenth Amendment's protection of only "male" voters gave states clear legal authority to disenfranchise women.

This left advocates of female suffrage no other option than to insist that the next amendment guarantee their voting rights, also. Douglass sympathized; he was a lifelong advocate of women's suffrage and had even attended the legendary Seneca Falls Convention in 1848. But he thought it crucial to secure the freedmen's rights immediately, and including women in a constitutional amendment would almost certainly ensure defeat. Female suffrage was an argument for another day.

This disagreement with feminists—many of whom had been fellow laborers in the anti-slavery cause—turned ugly. "Shall American statesmen . . . so amend their constitutions as to make their wives and mothers the political inferiors of unlettered and unwashed ditch-diggers, bootblacks, butchers, and barbers, fresh from the slave plantations of the south?" asked Elizabeth Cady Stanton at an 1869 convention. To give black men the vote before white women would be "[t]o exalt ignorance above education, vice above virtue, brutality and barbarism above refinement and religion."[27] Douglass's reply was equally vehement. "I do not see how any one can pretend that there is the same urgency in giving the ballot to woman as to the negro," he answered. "When women, because they are women, are hunted down through the cities . . . ; when they are dragged from their houses and hung upon lamp-posts; when their children are torn from their arms and their brains dashed out upon the pavement; when they are objects of insult and outrage at every turn . . . they will have an urgency to obtain the ballot equal to our own."[28]

In 1870, the Fifteenth Amendment was ratified, promising protection for voting rights regardless of race, but allowing states to disenfranchise women. Douglass nevertheless rejoiced. "We have a future; everything is possible to us!"[29] Yet, southern states were recalcitrant, and the federal government's will to enforce civil rights there seemed to be waning already. The inauguration of Ulysses

Grant in 1869 should have ended Johnson's obstructionism, and at first it did. But gradually it became clear that the nation had little enthusiasm for the heavy burdens of protecting the freedmen.

Two decades earlier, when Douglass decided that the Garrisonian boycott on politics was a prideful way of elevating one's own moral purity over the messy but productive scrum of legislative debate, the Garrisonians had replied that political engagement would only accomplish half-measures, lend credibility to the enemies of justice, and squander Douglass's moral advantage. The federal government seems to have spent much of the rest of the century trying to prove them right. Time and again, the old Confederacy refused to honor the Thirteenth, Fourteenth, and Fifteenth Amendments; and although the White House initially tried to enforce them, it gradually backed down until the color line was again firmly established.

An early hint of the disrespect Douglass would be forced to endure came in 1871, when he was asked to serve as secretary to a delegation that Grant dispatched to the Dominican Republic. The president, hoping to annex the island nation to the United States, sent three prominent Republican leaders to inspect the area, meet with local officials, and write up a report. Douglass, who favored annexation, was delighted at the opportunity to accompany them. Yet when the mission was over, the three excluded him from their debriefings with the president. Douglass voiced his sense of betrayal privately to his friend Charles Sumner, but to the president himself, he said nothing.

Sumner was already convinced that Grant was "essentially unjust,"[30] but Douglass remained loyal. In 1872, he traveled to New Orleans to preside over the Negro Labor Convention, which was essentially a Republican Party rally. In retrospect, the site of the convention seems metaphorical. Louisiana was experiencing a miniature civil war of its own, and New Orleans was ground zero for some of the worst violence of the period. The gubernatorial contest that year ended in dispute—which led to the impeachment of the incumbent for mishandling the election. The last month of his term was finished by P.B.S. Pinchback, who thereby became the state's first black governor. At last, the Republican candidate William Pitt Kellogg was proclaimed the winner, but his Democratic opponent, a former Confederate officer named John McEnery, refused to back down.

Claiming to be the state's legitimate governor, McEnery formed a rump legislature and spent several months presiding over a rival government in New Orleans. The two men's supporters clashed throughout the state, most infamously in the April 1873 Colfax Massacre, the deadliest single incident of Reconstruction-era violence, which resulted in the deaths of about 150 black Louisianans. In September 1874, McEnery's paramilitary White Man's League mustered 5,000 soldiers to overthrow Kellogg, and the ensuing "Battle of Liberty Place" ended in McEnery's victory. Federal troops chased his soldiers away days later but were forced to stay in the city for years to keep order. The quarrel reached Washington when Louisiana Democrats disputed the credentials of Pinchback, who had been elected to the Senate by Kellogg's Republican supporters. Senate leaders referred that matter to a committee, which dragged its feet for nearly four years.

That was all in the future when Douglass led the New Orleans conventioneers in pledging support for Grant's reelection. The convention did not even insist that Republicans include a civil rights plank in their party platform.[31] Whatever the party's flaws, Douglass thought it was the freedmen's only sensible option. It was the ship, he said; all the rest was the stormy sea. Yet, Republican compromises continued, and the party seemed to prioritize reconciliation among whites over justice for blacks. That policy seemed perfectly articulated in Grant's lazy slogan, "let us have peace," a phrase incessantly invoked during these years as an excuse for letting bygones be bygones among whites and ignoring the racial crimes of the past.

"Yes, let us have peace, but let us have liberty, law, and justice first," Douglass thundered back. "Let us have the Constitution, with its thirteenth, fourteenth, and fifteenth amendments fairly interpreted, faithfully executed, and cheerfully obeyed."[32] But the party continued to retreat from its duties toward formerly enslaved citizens, and in 1876, when the presidential election ended in a tie, Republican candidate Rutherford B. Hayes reached a deal with Democrats. In exchange for the presidency, he would withdraw union troops from the South, effectively ending Reconstruction. The agreement was a "withering blast," Douglass wrote, and the Hayes years "were, to the loyal colored citizen, full of darkness and dismal terror."[33]

Having nowhere else to go, Douglass remained a Republican and tried to put a positive spin on news whenever possible, particularly emphasizing the accomplishments of himself and other freedmen as proof of the progress of equality. But there was no denying that that the pace of improvement was slowing, and his lectures and writings took on an increasingly bleak tone from this time forward. "We cannot be asking too much," he wrote in one article pleadingly entitled "Give Us the Freedom Intended for Us." "We are not free. We cannot be free without the appropriate legislation provided for [to enforce the Thirteenth, Fourteenth, and Fifteenth Amendments]."[34]

Two personal tragedies worsened his growing sense of failure. The first was the burning of his Rochester home in 1872, which destroyed, among other things, his collection of the full run of *Frederick Douglass' Paper*—the only such collection in existence. Douglass moved his family to Washington, D.C. Then, two years later, he was induced to accept the position of president of the Freedman's Bank, which he only later learned was insolvent. Congress had chartered the bank a decade previously with the goal of supporting black entrepreneurs and boosting black property ownership. But conflicts of interest on its board and a deep recession in 1873 ruined the bank's credibility. Its leaders recruited

Douglass in hopes of restoring public confidence. Persuaded at first that the bank could reverse its fortunes, he assured Congress that depositors would be paid dollar for dollar, and even lent the bank $10,000 of his own money. But only months later, when he discovered just how perilous the situation was, he reported to the Senate that the bank could not be saved, and its doors were soon closed.

He had no hand in wrongdoing, but the episode was personally humiliating, and he spent an entire chapter in his final memoir exonerating himself. Far more than wrongful accusations of false dealing, Douglass was pained by the idea that he had been a part of an institution that betrayed the trust of poor and struggling workers. But worse betrayals were on the horizon.

# 8. The Fraud: 1876–1884

The virtual reestablishment of slavery in the South in the form of Jim Crow and the Klan was so horrific a prospect that Douglass spent much of this rest of his life alternately denouncing it with the terrific might of his eloquence and pretending it wasn't happening. His everlasting faith in the principles of the Declaration of Independence and the protections promised by the Constitution made it impossible for him to give up on the potential of a colorblind America. And there were at first real gains for the former slaves and their children, which he could justly celebrate. Many of those gains were to him personally in the form of wealth and status, and he tried to use them as a platform from which to hurl down wrath upon the racism that remained.

That came with a cost, however: his effectiveness as a spokesman for equality was enhanced so much by his political prestige that he periodically muffled himself to maintain that prestige. Yet, at other times he became more vocal in denouncing postwar racism. In retrospect, he seems to have alternated between the roles of iconoclastic radical and devout traditionalist. Toward the end of his life, he even called emancipation itself a fraud—while reiterating his devotion to America's founding principles.

Thus, just as Douglass defies the modern categories of "liberal" and "conservative," he also occupies a middle ground between the two magnetic poles of 20th-century black politics: Booker T. Washington and W. E. B. DuBois. On the one hand, Washington, like Douglass, was born a slave. He knew Douglass personally and even wrote one of the earliest biographies of him. Like Douglass, Washington focused his energies on self-improvement and self-reliance, and on the responsibilities of citizenship and hard work. Yet, Douglass would probably have scorned Washington's "accomodationist" view that counseled blacks to be patient regarding segregation and not to pursue political remedies.[1] On the other hand, while Douglass would have had no truck with DuBois's racial separatism, his renunciation of American citizenship, or his admiration for Josef Stalin, it was the wealthy and refined DuBois who became, before the ascent of Martin Luther King Jr., the 20th century's foremost spokesman for political activism in the Douglass mode. Compared with more recent black leaders, Douglass stands apart: like Malcolm X, he repudiated the nonviolence that King embraced; but like King, he would have rejected the black nationalism associated with Malcolm.

Such seeming paradoxes are more an artifact of today's narrow-minded political classifications than of any inconsistencies on Douglass's part. His stern epigrams about self-reliance, as well as his belief that black Americans should devote themselves to "well directed, honest toil"[2] and his scorn for the notion of black pride as "a positive evil,"[3] seem conservative nowadays, perhaps even insensitive. "I can't really imagine a radical progressive, today, saying [as Douglass did] 'Food to the indolent is poison, not sustenance,'" wrote Ta-Nehisi Coates in 2011.[4] But such words were simply reiterations of Douglass's longstanding belief in the sanctity of the individual and his hostility to any political system that offered to care for people in exchange for their surrendering their freedom. Politically, his creed of small-government self-reliance has more in common with the views of such black intellectuals as columnist Thomas Sowell, economist Walter Williams, or Supreme Court Justice Clarence Thomas— who keeps a portrait of Douglass on his office wall and regularly quotes him in his opinions—than those of contemporary social justice activists of the left.

This may explain a troubling thread in Douglass scholarship that claims he had a "hopeless secret desire to be white" or to "blot out his blackness,"[5] and that his emphasis on "optimism . . . patience . . . hard work, saving . . . accumulating property . . . sound morality, good character, and the value of education and knowledge" amounted to urging blacks to become "like whites."[6] Douglass would have been scandalized at the notion that embracing such virtues manifests a desire to be white. He did not long to change his race; he longed for a raceless world. "My cause, first, midst, last, and always," he wrote, "was and is that of the black man; not because he is black, but because he is a man."[7] Pride in one's own race was in his eyes no less "ridiculous" than hatred of other races.[8] The values he emphasized were good for the individual, and his hope was that Americans would learn to focus on the quality of each man and woman specifically, rather than on skin color, and thereby make racism obsolete. Certainly he would have rejected Ta-Nehisi Coates's belief that "racism remains, as it has since 1776, at the heart of this country's political life." On the contrary, Douglass believed the nation's heart was the principle of equality articulated in the Declaration of Independence, and that to assert the contrary was to concede the claims of white supremacists.[9]

Douglass was, of course, under no illusions about the racism that permeated American society in his day. He was all too aware that practices such as sharecropping, the payment of laborers with scrip redeemable at company stores instead of with cash, and the boycotting of black businesses by white customers had effects as insidious as those of legislated Jim Crow.[10] He excoriated labor unions for admitting only white members as a means of limiting competition for jobs. Recognizing that black entrepreneurs were often excluded from access to capital, he hoped the Freedman's Bank would extend a helping hand. And he spoke out against the racist code whereby police and prosecutors often minimized or ignored law breaking by whites while jailing or lynching black men for even minor or imaginary infractions. When combined with overtly racist laws, the social mores of the resurrected white supremacist culture amounted to a "new crusade against the Negro."[11]

Thus, while he rejected the racial separatism or race-pride approaches offered by other black leaders, Douglass nevertheless emphasized that discriminatory enforcement, disparate punishment, lack of access to education and economic opportunity, and indoctrination into racist ideology were all reinforcing the color line and leading to de facto reenslavement. In his condemnations of his era's social and structural inequalities, Douglass was the equal of any modern progressive.

Far from being a conservative, Douglass looked forward to a social revolution. He sought, as scholar Nicholas Buccola writes, nothing short of "a refounding of the American republic in a way that vindicated the first principles expressed in the Declaration of Independence and purged it of beliefs and practices offensive to those principles."[12] This was an ultimately radical prospect, and it entitles Douglass to a place among America's Founding Fathers as one of the creators of the nation as we now know it. On the spectrum between Washington and DuBois, Douglass might best be described as using DuBois's methods toward Washington's ends: black political activism was to him an indispensable means to the pursuit of happiness and self-reliance, and to peace, security, and freedom without regard to race.

These radical goals were often in tension with Douglass's need for institutional credibility—a constant temptation to compromise that dogs anyone who participates in politics. That tension burst forth in 1876, when the Senate committee ruled at last on P. B. S. Pinchback's election as senator from Louisiana four years before. Republicans cast the deciding votes to reject his credentials. Douglass was furious. "I think that they have acted from first to last under the influences of a mean and malignant prejudice of race. The very air of the country is pervaded by this prejudice."[13] Yet, when the Hayes administration, in an effort to defuse criticism for abandoning Reconstruction, offered Douglass a job as U.S. marshal for the District of Columbia, he accepted. It was certainly an honor, except that the administration simultaneously ended the tradition of having the marshal introduce the president to visitors at White House ceremonies. That was not one of the marshal's *official* duties—just a tradition—but it was plain that the change was made to avoid forcing presidential guests to endure the company of a black man.

Douglass nevertheless chose not to resign. When he was condemned in the press for submitting to such an insult, he insisted that there was no offense in it. The president, he said, had the right to decide who would introduce him "for reasons that must have been satisfactory to his judgment," and to quit over such a slight would have made him seem "foolish and ridiculous."[14] But this was rationalizing. The fact was that Douglass, once so attentive to his dignity that he seemed touchy, was now willingly participating in an obvious sham designed to defang condemnation of the Compromise of 1877. And the criticism he got for it stung. As Booker T. Washington wrote, Douglass "was always sensitive to the least evidence of opposition or slight on the part of his own people."[15]

He may have tried to compensate for a feeling of personal guilt by increasing the pace and heat of his rhetoric. He went on a speaking tour of the Midwest, between Kansas and Ohio, up through Pennsylvania, then through New York to Washington, denouncing the rising tide of violence and racism in the South. In June 1877, he went to Baltimore to view the sites of his childhood and visit old acquaintances, including his former master, the dying Thomas Auld. The unfeeling tyrant of his youth was now a withered and bedridden old man, and Marshal Douglass could afford to be magnanimous. Southerners tried to paint the reunion as a former slave seeking forgiveness; in fact, it was Douglass, a worldwide celebrity and national hero, who condescended to notice a commonplace invalid who is remembered today only because he once owned Douglass's bones and muscles.[16]

A year later, Douglass's rhetoric was in full force in New York City when he delivered one of his best orations, "There Was a Right Side in the Late War." The reconciliation policies of the past decade were perverting historical memory, he warned. In their desire for rapprochement with the white South, northern whites were viewing it as a merely sectional conflict rather than a show-down over the greatest of principles. Yet, "the sectional character of this war was merely accidental" and its "least significant fea-ture." The Civil War had been "a war of ideas . . . between the old and new, slavery and freedom, barbarism and civilization; between a government based upon the broadest and grandest declaration of human rights the world ever heard or read, and another pretended government, based upon an open, bold, and shocking denial of all rights."[17] It was fine to be magnanimous, but it was too much to ask Americans to overlook the cruel in-justices the Confederates fought to perpetuate. "I admit that the South believed it was right, but the nature of things is not changed by belief. . . . There was a right side and a wrong side in the late war, which no sentiment ought to cause us to forget." It was "no part of our duty to confound right with wrong, or loyalty with treason."[18]

When James Garfield was inaugurated in 1881, Marshal Douglass participated in the ceremonies, escorting the new presi-dent to take his oath of office. He admired Garfield and was hon-ored to be invited to the White House to discuss the president's plans to appoint black officers to the government. Douglass liked the idea. "It would say to the country and the civilized world that the great Republican party . . . was an honest party, and meant all it had said, and was determined hereafter to take no step back-ward."[19] But he doubted Garfield had the fortitude to compete against southern intransigence on civil rights. When the president was assassinated a few months later, the question was rendered moot. His successor, Chester Arthur, was far worse. Arthur did not renew Douglass's tenure as marshal but gave him instead the remunerative but insultingly trivial job of Recorder of Deeds for the District of Columbia. Douglass thought the new president's "self-indulgence, indifference, and neglect of opportunity, allowed the country to drift (like an oarless boat in the rapids) toward the howling chasm of the slaveholding Democracy."[20]

The reign of racist terrorism, especially but not exclusively in the South, was steadily worsening. In 1882, 49 black Americans were lynched; the next year, 53. The number rose to a peak of 161 in 1892—almost one every other day. Meanwhile, southern states disenfranchised and disarmed black citizens, and the number of black officeholders dwindled. When North Carolina Rep. George Henry White retired in 1901, he proved to be the last black southern representative in Congress until 1972. Throughout the 1880s and '90s, Douglass's disillusionment grew until it almost doused his faith in the national soul. Yet, he never entirely gave in to cynicism. "The sky of the American Negro is dark, but not rayless," he said in 1883. Although the Republican policy of "[p]eace with the old master class has been war to the Negro," there was still reason for hope. "The moral government of the universe is on our side, and cooperates, with all honest efforts, to lift up the down-trodden."[21]

For many, that hope seemed too far away to justify waiting. Beginning in about 1879, freedmen began to move north and west in large numbers, especially to Kansas. These migrants came to be known as the "Exodusters," and many prominent black leaders encouraged their flight. In fact, Douglass was virtually alone in opposing the movement, which he did with his full weight. Bad as conditions might be for blacks in the South, he insisted they should stay and fight. They were still better off there—where they were concentrated enough to exert political influence, where their labor was more in demand, and where they had the moral high ground—than in northern or western communities where they had no such resources. Advocates of migration were dangling before the eyes of poor and uneducated farmers a "dazzling" but false promise of "a land abounding, if not in 'milk and honey,' certainly in pork and hominy."[22] Moving also meant acquiescing in the federal government's refusal to protect civil rights in the South.

Such arguments were unrealistic to struggling sharecroppers whose lives and freedoms were being systematically ripped away. Paper promises of civil rights meant nothing to them. And the advice of the Hon. Frederick Douglass—who lived in a comfortable home on Cedar Hill in Anacostia, with a lovely view of the Washington Monument—may have been hard to take. The migration west and north continued. By 1888, Douglass himself had changed his mind; after visiting the Deep South, he announced his support for the Exodusters.

Douglass was right at least that the Exoduster movement was, in one sense, only postponing the nation's inevitable and necessary reckoning with racism. "Large bodies move slowly," he warned. "Individuals may be converted on the instant and change their whole course of life. Nations never. Time and events are required for the conversion of nature."[23] Given the persistence of racism and slavery in human history, the wonder was that so much progress had been made so quickly. "If liberty, with us, is yet but a name, our citizenship is but a sham, and our suffrage thus far only a cruel mockery, we may yet congratulate ourselves upon the fact that the laws and institutions of the country are sound, just and liberal." In time, those institutions would wash away prejudice, and "the color line will ultimately become harmless."[24] There could be no shortcuts.

In 1882, Douglass's wife Anna died at the age of 69. Whatever the state of their marriage had been, the 65-year-old Douglass was genuinely grieved at her loss. And his depression was worsened by the nation's increasing refusal to defend the rights of the black man. At a convention in Kentucky a year later, he listed the demands of "the six millions of colored people of this country" who were being excluded systematically from the American dream.[25] They wanted nondiscriminatory education; an end to racial exclusion from labor unions and to the payment system that fostered sharecropping; the honoring of payments to black veterans; reimbursement for depositors who lost money in the Freedman's Bank; and, most of all, faithful enforcement of the Civil Rights Act of 1875.

That act was the final achievement of Sen. Charles Sumner, whose last words had been a plea to see it passed through Congress. It prohibited discrimination in hotels, theaters, restaurants, and other places of public accommodation. But southerners claimed it violated their private property rights to force them to do business with people they despised. To Douglass, that argument misrepresented what the act really required. "A man's house is his castle," he acknowledged, "and he has a right to admit or refuse admission to it as he may please." But whenever a person "goes upon the public street," he "has the right to walk, ride, and be accommodated with food and shelter in a public conveyance or hotel." The government could not forcibly eliminate racism and should not try. Rather, "each individual man and woman" had to learn to look beyond color. But the government had made a sacred promise to protect the rights of all Americans regardless of race.[26]

Only a month after Douglass spoke, however, the Supreme Court dealt that promise a serious blow when it invalidated a major portion of the act in a decision called the *Civil Rights Cases*.[27] The justices declared that the federal ban on discrimination exceeded Congress's powers, because the Fourteenth Amendment barred only state governments from discriminating; it gave Congress no authority to outlaw discrimination by private businesses. The lone dissenter was Justice John Harlan, who years later would dissent in the infamous *Plessy v. Ferguson*. Douglass, mercifully, did not live to see that decision, but the *Civil Rights Cases* were painful enough. The ruling foreswore federal protections

93

that, however neglected, had at least offered a lodestar for constitutional rights. Now, there was little Douglass could point to as proof that a better day was coming.

He told the audience at a Washington, D.C., protest meeting that he could not comprehend the Court's logic. "In the dark days of slavery," he said, referring to the *Dred Scott* case, "the *intention* of the law, it was said, must prevail." But now the Court had "made no account whatever of the intention and purpose of Congress and the president in putting the Civil Rights Bill upon the Statute Book of the Nation." Nor did it make sense to apply the constitutional ban on discrimination only to government officials and not private citizens. "As individuals, the people of the State of South Carolina may stamp out the rights of the Negro wherever they please, so long as they do not do so as a State. All the parts can violate the Constitution, but the whole cannot. . . . What does it matter to a colored citizen that a State may not insult and outrage him, if a citizen of a State may? The effect upon him is the same."[28] Not until 1964 would Congress impose meaningful limits on discrimination by private businesses.

In January 1884, Douglass proved once again his own rejection of the color line when he remarried, this time to a white woman. His bride was 46-year-old Helen Pitts, who had done heroic work as a teacher in the post-war South, and was now serving as his clerk in his office as Recorder of Deeds and helping him revise his autobiography. The marriage came as a surprise to his children, and they did not take it well. None attended the wedding, and their relationship with their stepmother remained stiff to the last. Helen's family reacted no better: her parents, also well-known abolitionists, barred the door to their new son-in-law, and her father never spoke to her again. The public, white and black, shared their disgust. "We are opposed to colored men marrying second-rate white women," wrote black nationalist John Edward Bruce in a D.C. newspaper. "Barnum could make a mint of money out of this couple if they would consent to go on exhibition."[29]

As for the howls of white racists, Douglass could not help wryly noting that many of those who condemned him for marrying Helen "had remained silent over the unlawful relations of the white slave masters with their colored slave women" decades before.[30] He was, of course, himself the product of such a union. Yet, it hurt him that others—particularly his own children—never reconciled to the match. When journalist Ida B. Wells came to visit in 1892, he noted that she was "the only colored woman save [one] who has come into my home as a guest and has treated Helen as a hostess has a right to be treated." Shocked, Wells asked why others would disrespect her. "Well," he replied, "as many of her white friends had resented her marrying me, so my colored friends showed their resentment even in our home."[31]

But if friends and family made their disapproval clear, Douglass was impressed that Grover Cleveland, the first Democrat in the White House since the war, treated the couple with the greatest respect when they dined together in 1886. Cleveland's own marriage was unorthodox: earlier that year the 49-year-old president had married his best friend's daughter, 21-year-old Francis Folsom, who had been his ward since age 11 after his friend's death. Although the Republican Douglass was "separated" from the views of the Democrat Cleveland "by a space ocean wide," he reported that the president and his wife were entirely "cordial and courteous."[32]

# 9. Abroad: 1884–1895

Douglass retired from the "comfortable office" of Recorder of Deeds in 1886.[1] That fall, he and Helen began a year of travel which took them to England, France, Italy, and Egypt. He climbed to the top of one of the pyramids—an ordeal for a 77 year old man, and one he "paid dearly for."[2] Gazing out at the horizon, he experienced a moment of wonder at the thought of all the empires that had risen and fallen and all the changes he had witnessed in his own life. "A few years back my Sundays were spent on the banks of the Chesapeake Bay, bemoaning my condition and looking out from the farm of Edward Covey, and, with a heart aching to be on their decks, watching the white sails of the ships passing off to sea. Now I was enjoying what the wisest and best of the world have bestowed for the wisest and best to enjoy."[3]

Back in the United States for the election of 1888, he was called on to speak at the Republican Party's national convention. He had not supported the nominee, Benjamin Harrison, but he emphasized the need for party unity in the general election and for the "Grand Old Party" to hold true to its anti-slavery origin. Democrats, he warned, were united in their effort to reestablish slavery under another name, and Republicans still had it within their power to prevent such a travesty. That, indeed, was "the vital and animating principle of the Republican Party."[4] Southerners accused Republicans of "waving the bloody shirt" when they reminded audiences that Democrats had supported slavery and secession, but Douglass was undeterred. "Let that shirt be waved as long as there shall be a drop of innocent blood upon it."[5]

The Republicans won that year, and in 1889, Harrison offered Douglass the position of consul-general to the Republic of Haiti. It was the greatest honor of his life.[6] His trip to the Dominican Republic as secretary to Grant's special mission in 1871 had ended in embarrassment, but this time he would go as the equivalent of an ambassador (a title the United States did not use until 1893).

The appointment had tremendous symbolic importance as well. Haiti had been the site of the 1791 uprising by slaves led by Toussaint L'Ouverture, a revolt that terrified U.S. slaveholders and made L'Ouverture a hero to those who dreamt of slaves seizing their own freedom. For a century, the small nation had struggled against overwhelming odds—even defying the armies of Napoleon—to maintain its independence. Despite poverty and political turbulence, it became, in the words of slavery historian David Brion Davis, "a harbinger of universal emancipation."[7] The slave Denmark Vesey, executed in South Carolina in 1822 for planning a revolt, had worked in Haiti; and David Walker, who published his anti-slavery *Appeal* a few years later, pointed to Haiti as "the glory of the blacks and terror of tyrants."[8] For their part, many Haitians idolized Douglass.

By the time of Douglass's appointment, however, the age of empire had begun, and the small Caribbean nations were fearful of annexation. During the Grant years, Douglass had supported union with Haiti, but conditions had changed, thanks to a coup led by Generals Louis Mondestin Florvil Hyppolite and François Denys Légitime. After their rebellion succeeded, Légitime claimed the presidency, only to have his former comrade turn against him. Hyppolite asked American arms merchants for help, but their shipments were unable to penetrate a naval blockade that Légitime established around the island. At last, the U.S. Navy helped the weapons get through, and with the American guns in hand, Hyppolite's forces drove Légitime into exile. Soon it was rumored that Hyppolite had promised to repay the Navy by handing over the Môle St. Nicolas, a port important not only for refueling naval vessels but also because it was the location of the undersea cable that controlled Haiti's communications with the outside world.

Consul-General Douglass was never instructed to negotiate for the acquisition of Môle St. Nicolas, however, and when the subject came up, President Harrison seemed unenthusiastic about any such transfer. The Haitian public opposed the idea, fearing it would give the United States a foothold to take over the country, and Hyppolite simply left the issue alone. Thus, for nearly a year, the new diplomat attended receptions and handled correspondence with no movement being made by the American government or the Hyppolite regime toward transferring the port to U.S. control. It was not until January 1891, that the subject was first broached by Secretary of State James G. Blaine in a letter to Douglass that announced that the government was sending someone to "assist" him in the negotiations. That someone was Admiral Bancroft Ghirardi, an arrogant and hardheaded military man with little of the grace needed for international relations. When he arrived, he made clear that the State Department expected him, not Consul-General Douglass, to lead the discussion. Two days later, when the Americans met with Hyppolite, Ghirardi did most of the talking. "My connection with this negotiation," Douglass wrote bitterly afterward, "was very humble, secondary and subordinate."[9]

He considered resigning, but stayed on to avoid embarrassing the administration. When the Haitian government asked the State Department to clarify what precise authority Admiral Ghirardi had, the department's answer—which did not arrive for two months—said only that he and Douglass had joint powers. Yet, the two Americans disagreed about the basis for the claim to the port. Ghirardi openly avowed that Hyppolite had promised it in exchange for breaking the Légitime blockade. That statement struck Douglass as a shameful admission that the U.S. government was a mercenary force that would "covertly [assist] in putting down one government and setting up another" in exchange for a direct payoff.[10] He preferred to base the claim to Môle St. Nicolas on the shared interests of Haiti and the United States and on the principles of "good neighborhood and advanced civilization."[11] Worse, Ghirardi thought the State Department's instructions required them to ask Haiti for an exclusive deal, while Douglass thought the instructions left them free to sign an agreement even if Haiti also let other navies use the port.

They tried both routes. But Hyppolite's government had resolved not to lease the port at all, thanks partly to New York newspapers boasting that Môle St. Nicolas was just the first step toward an outright seizure of Haiti, and partly to watching Admiral Ghirardi's fleet sail around the Caribbean for months—an effort at intimidation that only stiffened the Haitians' opposition to imperialism. In May 1891, Douglass was forced to inform Washington that Hyppolite had ended the talks.

Not long afterward, Douglass and his wife were alarmed at the sound of gunfire when an uprising burst upon the Haitian capital. Hyppolite's government put the rebellion down with massacres and torture. But the violence, combined with a dangerous illness that Helen contracted around that time and cruel attacks in the American press over his alleged bungling of the negotiations, led Douglass to resign that July. He printed a long and persuasive defense of his conduct in the *North American Review*, but hovering over the whole affair was the bitter feeling that the administration had sent Ghirardi in the first place because it was reluctant to trust a black man with the burdens of diplomacy. Failure was probably inevitable—and was doubtless more the consequence of Haitian politics than any fault of the Americans—yet newspapers found it easy to make Douglass a scapegoat.

Of all the tributes heaped on Douglass during his lifetime, he said, two stood out: his appointment to Haiti and the request from Hyppolite, made a few months after his return to the United States, that he represent that country at the World's Columbian Exposition, better known as the Chicago World's Fair.

The fair, which opened to the public in May 1893, commemorated the anniversary of Columbus's landing in the New World with a six-month spectacle of art and architecture from different countries. Douglass was enough of a celebrity to draw a large crowd to his lecture, "Haiti and the Haitian People." Among the attendees was the young poet Paul Laurence Dunbar, who had just published his first book. He read Douglass his "Ode to Ethiopia" ("Be proud, my race, in mind and soul;/Thy name is writ on Glory's scroll/In characters of fire."), which Douglass much admired.

But black Americans soon realized that the fair almost entirely neglected them—or worse. It was considered unremarkable that James D. Lynch, a lawyer and versifier from Mississippi who was best known for an epic poem praising the Klan, was named the fair's poet laureate. And many of the fair's scholarly displays oozed with condescending racist anthropology. The Smithsonian's curator, Otis T. Mason, put together an ethnological exhibit that detailed what he called "the three modern types of savagery, namely: the American [Indian], the Negroid, and the Malayo-Polynesian."[12] Worse still, the fair set aside August 25 as "Colored People's Day"—not a respectful exhibition of black Americans' contributions to world culture, but a minstrel-show parody at which 2,500 watermelons were handed out to the crowd. Some of Douglass's friends proposed a boycott, and many stayed away.

A disgusted Douglass went home, but he returned in the afternoon to present his lecture, "The Race Problem in America," to a massive audience. Although he had been delivering that address for years, the elderly Douglass seemed thrown off when hecklers began shouting as he read from his manuscript. But after a pause he laid aside his notes and the old majesty of his abolition oratory seemed reborn. "There is no Negro problem," he boomed. "The problem is whether the American people have honesty enough, loyalty enough, honor enough, patriotism enough, to live up to their own Constitution." Black soldiers had died on the field of honor to save the country from treason. "Have you forgotten that now?" The fair's organizers were determined to portray black Americans as savages not far removed from the villages of Africa. "But stop. Look at the progress the negro has made in thirty years!" The freedmen—and now their children, who were coming of age—"intend that the American people shall learn the great lesson of the brotherhood of man and the fatherhood of God from our presence among them."[13] Dunbar closed the session by reciting a poem, probably "The Colored Soldiers."[14]

Dunbar was not the venerable Douglass's only protégé. Douglass was so impressed by the young journalist Ida B. Wells's coverage of lynching in the South that he took the train to New York to meet her. "Brave woman!" he wrote later. "You have done your people and mine a service which can neither be weighed nor measured."[15] The two worked together on a pamphlet decrying the Chicago Fair's disparagement of blacks. Wells considered Douglass "the greatest man our race has produced,"[16] and his sponsorship proved an important aid to her career.

That autumn, with the fair coming to a close, Douglass visited Wells's office at the Chicago *Conservator* and invited her to lunch. There was a nice restaurant across the street, she told him, but it served only whites. "Mr. Douglass, in his vigorous way, grasped my arm and said, 'Come, let's go there.'" When the couple entered, "[t]he waiters seemed paralyzed," so Douglass chose a table and pulled out a chair for Wells. The owner appeared and, as soon as he recognized Douglass, lost his frown and summoned a waiter to take their order while he gushed over his famous guest. "Ida," Douglass finally muttered, "I thought you said that they didn't serve us here. It seems we are getting more attention than we want and I have no chance to talk to you."[17]

Young intellectuals like Wells and Dunbar gave Douglass the hope he needed at a time when the fortunes of black Americans were receding dramatically. In just the previous decade, lynchings of blacks had more than tripled. In February 1892, a mob of nearly 1,000 whites dragged 32-year-old Edward Coy from a Texarkana jail, tied him to a stake, and skinned him before burning him to death for allegedly raping a white woman. A year later, 17-year-old Henry Smith was burned at the Paris, Texas, fairgrounds before an audience of perhaps 15,000 people. Railroad companies scheduled special trains to carry viewers wanting to witness it. The federal government did nothing.

What the future would hold for black Americans nobody could know, but the horizon seemed bleak, and some prominent leaders were not confident that the new generation was prepared for the struggle. Around the same time that he met Wells and Dunbar, Douglass was invited to speak at the Tuskegee Institute by its president, the star-struck Booker T. Washington. Douglass delivered his popular "Self-Made Men" lecture, emphasizing self-improvement, education, and hard work. It was a message that Washington, of course, wholeheartedly embraced. Yet despite his awe of Douglass, he privately feared that the great man's focus on self-improvement wasn't enough. The children of the freedmen "needed something more than to be reminded of their sufferings and of their political rights," Washington thought. "They needed to do something more than merely to defend themselves." But he thought Douglass was "not prepared" to undertake "the equally difficult task of fitting the Negro for the opportunities and responsibilities of freedom."[18]

Washington's prominence as an educator and reformer grew in the years that followed, to the point that some regarded him as Douglass's natural successor. Still, it seemed to others—particularly Washington's famous antagonist, W. E. B. DuBois—that white society accepted Washington only because he seemed willing to surrender the demand for equal treatment.

Just months after Douglass's death, Washington gave his notorious Atlanta address telling white America, "In all things that are purely social we can be as separate as the fingers, yet one as the hand in all things essential to mutual progress."[19] DuBois at first applauded the speech, but a few years later he unleashed a ripping attack on Washington for his apparent acceptance of segregation. DuBois's words continue to reverberate to this day. In one of his most effective passages, he pointed to Douglass, "the greatest of American Negro leaders," as a contrast. The old man had prioritized "the assertion of the manhood rights of the Negro by himself" in a way that Washington's conciliatory approach did not. "Douglass, in his old age, still bravely stood for the ideals of his early manhood,—ultimate assimilation *through* self-assertion, and on no other terms," wrote DuBois. But Washington was "a compromiser" who promoted "submission" and who "practically accepts the alleged inferiority of the Negro races." He was "essentially the leader not of one race but of two."[20]

Other writers also condemned Washington for apparently yielding what Douglass had fought so hard to maintain. One likened him to Benedict Arnold.[21] Another wrote that while "Douglass was like a lion, bold and fearless," Washington was "lamblike, meek and submissive."[22] Some scholars and activists still scorn Washington today, but as historian Robert Norrell argues, that view is unfair not just to Washington, but to DuBois and Douglass as well, because it tends to caricature their views and the complexities of their times. Washington was far more active in opposing segregation than today's scholars tend to recognize: he financed lawsuits, denounced lynching and segregation, and worked constantly for civil rights, as much as he was able.[23] But he thought conditions at the time rendered any more overt political approach hopeless.

Considering the events of the day, it is hard to disagree. Times had indeed changed, and Douglass's style of open protest was unlikely to work in the new era. Only a year after Washington's "hand" speech, the Supreme Court ratified "separate but equal" in *Plessy v. Ferguson*, and the promise of the post–Civil War world seemed virtually dead. Douglass and Wells might break up segregation in a Chicago eatery, but an ordinary farmer who tried to do the same in any rural Mississippi coffee shop might very well be murdered.

Thus, when DuBois, a Harvard-educated northerner, advocated the "talented tenth" strategy, which proposed to train a select group of black leaders to serve as the intellectual vanguard of an anti-segregation movement, Washington, born a slave and living in Alabama, demurred. He thought the crucial need at the time was for industrial education, to build a robust black middle class that could eventually afford to support an intellectual leadership: "The opportunity to earn a dollar in a factory just now is worth infinitely more than the opportunity to spend a dollar in an opera house."[24] That was a realistic opinion, given the increasing pace of racist terror in the United States and the overwhelming political advantages enjoyed by the enemies of civil rights.

The split between DuBois and Washington was not as much a difference of principle as it was a disagreement between allies about tactics, one that resembled the split between Douglass and Garrison decades before. Such internecine disputes are often the bitterest. Understandably, the colossal scale of the injustices they faced made some people long for Douglass's older style of uncompromising leadership. Yet, the simple fact was that black Americans were in a tragic position in the 1890s, and they had no solution within their grasp. Douglass may have been a lion, but as Norrell concludes, Washington was not a lamb—he was a fox, seeking clever ways to accomplish his ends short of direct confrontation, which would have been futile anyway.[25]

The type of direct protest DuBois advocated can be effective when conditions are right, but less overt tactics are more effective at other times, as Douglass himself recognized. In 1903, Washington recommended that the black man "deport himself modestly in regard to political claims," because full equality would be "a matter of natural, slow growth, not an over-night, gourd-vine affair."[26] He was, in effect, channeling Douglass's 1889 advice that racism could be overcome only gradually, by "lives and acquirements which contradict and put to shame this narrow and malignant feeling." "Manly self-assertion" was "a power," Douglass wrote, but "modesty is also a power"—so long as it is "manifested without any touch of servility."[27]

That is not to say Douglass would have adopted an accommo-dationist tactic himself. But the decay of the nation's commitment to civil rights that motivated Washington's conciliatory tone—and drove DuBois to greater radicalism—hovered over Douglass's oratory and writing in his declining years, pulling him alternately between activism and righteousness on the one hand and a coun-sel for patience and self-improvement on the other. He knew there were good reasons for hope, but "the omens," he admitted, "are against me."[28] His frustration is evident in his last great speech, "The Lessons of the Hour," delivered at a Washington, D.C., church on January 9, 1894.

The talk was classic Douglass: alternately ironic and sincere, bitter and evenhanded, and focused resolutely on justice. He ac-knowledged that the "indications" were "not hopeful" for equal-ity.[29] Lynching was becoming more common, even in northern states, and federal guarantees for civil rights were simply not enforced. Some whites naively assumed that lynching was the consequence of a black crime wave, but in reality, it was not about crime at all. It was a ritualistic means of reinforcing the mores of white supremacy. Southerners were systematically taught an "absolute contempt" for the life of the black man, Douglass ex-plained. "A dead negro with them is a common jest."[30]

There was "nothing in the history of savages to surpass the blood chilling horrors and fiendish excesses perpetrated against the colored people by the so-called enlightened and Christian people of the South."[31] Yet, upstanding white northerners kept blaming the victims and excusing the perpetrators—all in an effort "to sacrifice friends in order to conciliate enemies," and "to surrender the constitution to the late rebels for the lack of moral courage to execute its provisions."[32] Such cowardice had "shaken my faith in the nobility of the nation."[33] Even the Supreme Court had "surrendered," and the Republican Party had become "a party of money rather than a party of morals." It seemed as though "the cause gained in war, is the cause lost in peace."[34]

Douglass was equally frustrated to find that some people were yet again reviving the old prewar canard of African colonization, including some black leaders. "All this native land talk is nonsense," Douglass roared. "The native land of the American negro is America. His bones, his muscles, his sinews, are all American. His ancestors for two hundred and seventy years have lived, and labored, and died on American soil, and millions of his posterity have inherited Caucasian blood."[35] Worse, the colonization idea tended "to throw over the negro a mantle of despair" and encouraged whites to ratchet up the persecution in hopes that blacks might leave the country.

Colonization was merely an evasion of responsibility for fixing the problem of racial oppression. The only real answer was for white Americans to abandon their prejudices, "cultivate kindness and humanity," and give effect to the Constitution and the demands of justice. Invoking the Declaration of Independence, Douglass sounded once more his lifelong theme:

> I would call to mind the sublime and glorious truths with which, at its birth, [the United States] saluted a listening world. Its voice then, was the trump of an archangel, summoning hoary forms of oppression and time honored tyranny, to judgment. Crowned heads heard it and shrieked. Toiling millions heard it and clapped their hands for joy. It announced the advent of a nation, based upon human brotherhood and the self-evident truths of liberty and equality. Its mission was the redemption of

the world from the bondage of ages. Apply these sublime and glorious truths to the situation now before you. Put away your race prejudice. Banish the idea that one class must rule over another. Recognize the fact that the rights of the humblest citizen are as worthy of protection as are those of the highest, and your problem will be solved . . . [and] your Republic will stand and flourish forever.[36]

Eight days after this lecture, 24-year-old John Buckner, accused of raping a white woman in St. Louis, was snatched from his parents' home and hanged on a bridge over the Meramec River in front of 100 witnesses. The coroner called it suicide.[37]

# 10. Legacy

Douglass remained active even in retirement. He was a fixture at important Washington events and received honorary degrees from Wilberforce and Berea Colleges. Some time in his seventies, he began studying German. He had accumulated an impressive library and would sit and read his favorites, Victor Hugo or Alexandre Dumas (who, he noted, was half black like himself), or write at his desk, play his violin, or walk the grounds of his Cedar Hill estate. He received a steady stream of visitors. Legend has it that when one idealistic young man asked Douglass what he should do with his life, the "Sage of Anacostia" replied simply, "Agitate! Agitate! Agitate!"[1]

Always the radical, he attended a women's suffrage meeting in Washington on February 20, 1895. As he had promised during the debate over the Fifteenth Amendment, he resolutely supported amending the Constitution to give women voting rights. He had even been nominated for the vice presidency by the Equal Rights Party when it ran Victoria Woodhull as its presidential candidate in 1872.[2] Now, the 77-year-old activist leaned on Susan B. Anthony as he walked to the platform to once again proclaim himself a "radical woman suffrage man."[3] Then, he returned home for dinner, having another lecture scheduled for 7:00 p.m. While he was describing his day to Helen—mimicking the other speakers as he always enjoyed doing—he suddenly collapsed. His death came swiftly, of cardiac arrest.

For three days, a line of mourners came to view the body at Cedar Hill. The funeral, at the Metropolitan African Methodist Episcopal Church on M Street in Washington, brought a crowd of thousands. Helen and Douglass's three children accompanied the body to Rochester where, again, crowds turned out to pay their respects. At last he was laid to rest there, at the city's Mt. Hope Cemetery.

Douglass's status in the American pantheon faded after his death, as race relations reached their nadir. Even those scholars who did write about him treated him primarily as an anti-slavery orator and activist rather than an author or intellectual. The final version of his autobiography sold well, but few regarded it as a significant contribution to American letters, and his original *Narrative* went out of print for a century. His writings and speeches were not published in a collected edition until 1950. Biographies by Charles Chesnutt and Booker T. Washington, as well as monuments and landmarks named for him, kept his memory alive, but the vitality of his thought was drowned out by Jim Crow.

Meanwhile, the injustices continued. The Supreme Court, having given its imprimatur to segregation with its 1896 *Plessy* ruling, sporadically struck down some of the more extreme instances of racist government actions—most notably invalidating race-based zoning in 1917.[4] But the Court largely ceased to pay attention to the plight of black Americans. The White House was also apathetic. After Theodore Roosevelt invited Booker T. Washington to dine with him at the White House in 1901, South Carolina Sen. Benjamin "Pitchfork" Tillman, a vocal advocate of lynching, fumed that the president's action "will necessitate our killing a thousand niggers in the South before they learn their place again."[5] But Roosevelt was not inclined to defend civil rights in any event. When a detachment of black soldiers was falsely accused of involvement in a bar fight in Brownsville, Texas, in 1906, he summarily discharged 167 of them rather than inquire into the facts.

The white supremacist resurgence at the dawn of the 20th century was aided in large part by what Douglass had feared as early as his 1878 speech, "There Was a Right Side in the Late War."

He had warned that by downplaying the moral clash between freedom and slavery that sparked the rebellion, the nation risked forgetting the lessons of the conflict—and ultimately opened the possibility of slavery's return. Within two decades, that had become a reality as southern leaders sought to vindicate the Confederacy. Throughout the late 19th century, they erected monuments to Confederate soldiers, founded organizations such as the Sons of Confederate Veterans, and added Confederate symbols to the flags of southern states.

Accompanying this symbolic resurrection of the Confederacy was a concerted effort to rewrite the war's history to serve the ideological goal of white supremacy—an effort that produced what today's historians call the "Lost Cause" theory of the war. This reactionary doctrine, which came to dominate the political science and history departments of respectable universities throughout the country, held that the war had not really been about slavery at all and that the enfranchisement of former slaves had been an immense mistake.[6] Confederate President Jefferson Davis, for instance, recast the conflict in his 1881 memoirs as a fight for freedom and southern self-government rather than a showdown over the principles of equality. Slavery, he wrote, "may have served as an *occasion*, it was far from being the *cause* of the conflict."[7] Indeed, it was really "irrelevant."[8] The *true* cause had been interference with the constitutional autonomy of the states. Southerners, he claimed, were resisting federal interference with local affairs and were thus seeking to defend freedom, not to undermine the Constitution.

This was a lie—in the antebellum period, southerners had sought *more* federal power, not less, in the form of nationwide enforcement of the Fugitive Slave Act and federal subsidies for slavery's expansion. And slavery, far from being "irrelevant," was so central to the Confederate cause that Davis's home state of Mississippi avowed, in the same document that announced secession, "Our position is thoroughly identified with the institution of slavery."[9] Confederate Vice President Alexander Stephens had even called it the "cornerstone" of the secessionist government.[10]

Yet even northern scholars embraced the Lost Cause theory. Historian Eric Foner notes, "Few interpretations of history have had such far-reaching consequences": the theory gave a respectable intellectual excuse for the virtual reinstatement of slavery.[11] Charles Edward Merriam, the first professor of political science at the University of Chicago, pronounced in his 1903 book, *A History of American Political Theories*, "From the standpoint of modern political science, the slaveholders were right," adding that political theory had come to reject the immature abolitionist notion that all people are naturally entitled to freedom.[12] Indeed, Merriam believed that political theory in his day was dominated by the ideas of the ultradefender of slavery, John C. Calhoun.

The Lost Cause theory gained a particular triumph in 1912 when Professor Woodrow Wilson was elected president. Born into a slaveholding family in 1856—his father was an outspoken proponent of slavery and a chaplain in the Confederate army—Wilson briefly studied law at the University of Virginia and then in North Carolina before becoming a member of the Georgia bar. He quit law soon after to study at Johns Hopkins University, in Douglass's own Baltimore, where he took his doctoral degree. At these schools, his mind was warmed by the still-smoldering embers of the Confederate intellectual class who—legally barred from holding public office—had gone into law or teaching, instead. Steeped in the constitutional and racial theories of the Confederacy, Wilson moved through his academic career, becoming a leading spokesman for the Progressive ideology that rejected the ideas of the Declaration of Independence and opted instead for the organic collectivism that was once the heart of the Confederate cause. The Declaration's classical liberalism, Wilson said, was "radically evil and corrupting" because "it holds that government is a matter of contract and deliberate arrangement" and "that the object of government is liberty."[13]

Like many academics, Wilson wrote Lost Cause theory into his books on American history and politics. Slavery, he claimed, was "not so dark a thing as it was painted," because slaves were generally "happy and well cared for."[14] He viewed secession as impractical but saw "clearly the force or the justice of States Rights" and paid "loving tribute to the virtues of the leaders of secession, to the purity of their purposes, to the righteousness of the cause which they thought they were promoting."[15]

Above all, he considered Reconstruction a travesty, and he blamed not the white supremacists but the leaders of Reconstruction, who "preferr[ed] the interests of their wards to the interests of peaceable, wholesome, and healing progress."[16] The freedmen had been "excited by a freedom they did not understand," were "bewildered and without leaders, and yet insolent and aggressive; sick of work, covetous of pleasure,—a host of dusky children untimely put out of school."[17] Their unjustified demand for equality had forced southern leaders to restore the old order. Wilson was a college friend of Thomas Dixon, whose novel *The Clansman* was a paean to the Ku Klux Klan. Wilson screened the film version of that novel—the racist 1915 blockbuster *Birth of A Nation*—at the White House. The film quoted Wilson's books in several scenes, and the president was reported to have loved it.[18]

As president, Wilson reinstituted the segregation of government employees. Federal buildings had to have separate restrooms and eating tables for black workers. When William Monroe Trotter, a cofounder of the NAACP and a prominent editor, met Wilson at the White House to protest, the scene turned into a burlesque of Douglass's meeting with Lincoln half a century before. "Only two years ago you were heralded as perhaps the second Lincoln," Trotter said. But while Wilson promised a "New Freedom" for whites, he seemed to be offering "a new slavery for your Afro-American fellow citizens." Wilson replied that segregation was not meant as an insult but simply "to prevent any kind of friction between the white employees and the Negro employees."

When Trotter balked, Wilson flew into a rage and ordered Trotter out of his office. "Your tone, sir, offends me. . . . You have spoiled the whole cause for which you came."[19]

In the summer of 1919, race riots in Arkansas, Illinois, Nebraska, New York, South Carolina, Tennessee, Texas, and elsewhere took hundreds of lives. The Ku Klux Klan, which had largely dissolved in the Reconstruction Era thanks to federal prosecutions, now returned, stronger than ever. In 1925, 25,000 members marched in white hoods down Pennsylvania Avenue. Seven years later, New Orleans city fathers added a new inscription to the Liberty Place Monument, erected decades earlier to honor the uprising that, among other things, led to P. B. S. Pinchback's exclusion from Congress. The new wording praised the memory of those who "recognized white supremacy in the south and gave us our state."

Eight months after Douglass's death, a boy was born to the Washington, D.C., family of William Le Pré Houston, the son of a former slave. The boy was named Charles, and, like his father, he studied law, graduating from Harvard in 1922. Charles Hamilton Houston then served as dean of the Howard University Law School before becoming special counsel to the NAACP, where he oversaw the organization's efforts to have *Plessy v. Ferguson* overruled. As part of that program he dispatched his protégé, the idealistic Thurgood Marshall, to initiate lawsuits in state and federal courts that would climax at last with the 1954 *Brown v. Board of Education* ruling, striking down school segregation. Marshall, like Douglass a Marylander, was a graduate of Baltimore's Frederick Douglass High School, where Douglass himself had given the commencement address in 1894.

At the dawn of the civil rights movement in the 1950s, attention returned at last to Douglass's cultural contribution to the United States. Today, he is rightly recognized as a prototypical American character: the ultimate "self-made man." Schoolchildren now regularly read his *Narrative*, which is celebrated as an American literary classic. Yet, in some ways, Douglass has still not received his due. No major motion picture of his life has ever been produced, for example, even though his tale is among the most dramatic in the nation's history.[20] And, perhaps because his narrative is so compelling and beautifully written, he has generally been remembered more for his personal story than for his impact on political and constitutional thought.

His most lasting influence may be his oratorical and writing style. His rhetorical approach drew on a rich literary background, interwoven with witty epigrams, all delivered with overwhelming dignity and fortitude, and calling the nation back to its better self: what historians called "the jeremiad," after the prophet Jeremiah, who urged the Hebrews to return to their original faith. Though Douglass was far from the only black orator of his day, he was, as David Blight says, "at the head of the black adaptation of this tradition in the nineteenth century," and contributed to what became the standard form of expression for subsequent generations of black leaders.[21] This persuasive and passionate technique drew on the Declaration of Independence, the Bible, patriotic poetry, and rhapsodic invocations of hope and progress, to express the American Dream more eloquently than ever before.

In the midst of World War II, 15-year-old Mike King—later to call himself Martin Luther King, Jr.—drew on this tradition with outstanding effect when he won an oratorical contest with an entry entitled "The Negro and the Constitution."[22] Speaking of the black soldiers who were then fighting the Nazis while facing segregation at home, King's words could easily have been written by Douglass: "Today thirteen million black sons and daughters of our forefathers continue the fight for the translation of the Thirteenth, Fourteenth, and Fifteenth amendments from writing on the printed page to an actuality. We believe with them that 'if freedom is good for any it is good for all,' that we may conquer southern armies by the sword, but it is another thing to conquer southern hate, that if the franchise is given to Negroes, they will be vigilant and defend even with their arms, the ark of federal liberty from treason and destruction by her enemies."[23] As a student, learning to preach by watching pastors at nearby churches, King imbibed the tradition to which Douglass had added a powerful strain. When he became a crusader for civil rights, his speaking style combined the zeal of the Southern Baptist tradition with the stentorian and romantic dialectic that Douglass helped construct.

This contribution, however, describes only a fraction of Douglass's achievement. He was an authentic genius, who through his own effort became the nation's foremost abolitionist, with the sole exception of William Lloyd Garrison. Yet he transcended Garrison. More than an orator, he was a scholar and an intellectual who went beyond mere "agitation." He delved into some of the most complicated legal issues of his day and articulated a principled defense of classical liberalism and individual rights for all Americans. Of the pro-Constitution abolitionists, he was by far the most effective, devoting his postwar career to realizing the principles of the Declaration of Independence for the freedmen and their descendants. As Douglass scholar Peter Myers concludes, he "produced the most powerful argument for the affirmation of those principles in the history of African American political thought."[24]

Douglass was the foremost opponent of the colonization schemes that were offered time and again by both black and white Americans in his day—people who, in his view, were ultimately ignoring the moral imperative of the U.S. Constitution. Separatism, he believed, was an evasion of, not a solution to, injustice—and civic engagement was more important than maintaining one's own moral sanctity. His unique contribution to American political philosophy is well summarized in the contrast between the mottos he and Garrison used for their newspapers. Instead of Garrison's call for separation, "no union with slaveholders," Douglass demanded equality: "All rights for all."

When Martin Luther King Jr., Thurgood Marshall, and others made their great breakthroughs for civil rights in the 1950s and '60s, they did so not in the Garrisonian mode of nonparticipation, but in the terms Douglass articulated: black Americans have the same right—and the same obligation—to pursue happiness that all other Americans have. "The Declaration of Independence is the ringbolt to the chain of your nation's destiny," said Douglass in 1852. "Stand by those principles, be true to them on all occasions, in all places, against all foes, and at whatever cost."[25]

Ironically, this very accomplishment may account for some of the neglect of Douglass's work as a public intellectual. Many 20th-century scholars came to view his classical liberal politics as obsolete or even foolhardy. One critic for instance, argued that his individualism and belief in private property rights "impeded his comprehension" of the race problem in his own day.[26] Another contended that "[Chief Justice] Taney was right" to say in *Dred Scott* that America's founders never meant to include black Americans when they said all men are created equal, and called Douglass's arguments to the contrary "naïve" and "illusory."[27]

Peter Myers, the foremost expert on Douglass's political philosophy, rejects such claims. In his view, Douglass was correct to see "the doctrine of human equality in natural, inalienable rights" as "the strongest possible foundation for free government and for opposition to slavery and white supremacy."[28] Those who regard Douglass as naive, writes Myers, and who agree with white supremacists that the American Dream was not meant for blacks, perpetuate a "spirit of alienation and disempowerment" that is both self-destructive and contrary to the moral truths at the heart of the American Constitution—truths to which Douglass pledged his life.[29]

Whatever the ultimate verdict on these arguments, they at least prove the continuing vitality and relevance of Douglass's thought. He believed above all else in the potential of the free individual. Within each of us is a sacred personal uniqueness,

117

one that can and will take responsibility for building a noble and beautiful future, if only our hands are untied. And he believed that the U.S. Constitution protected that freedom—which was why it deserved to be cherished and defended. A self-made man himself, he viewed America as a land of self-made people: a place where every person, white or black, male or female, had the right, and would someday have the freedom, to pursue life as he or she chose. "We have as a people no past and very little present, but a boundless and glorious future," he said in his "Self-Made Men" lecture. "Our mottoes are 'Look ahead!' and 'Go ahead!'. . . . In this respect, America is not only the exception to the general rule, but the social wonder of the world."[30] If only the nation would manifest that wonder for all her people, the possibilities for progress were limitless.

Thus, beginning with the principles of the Declaration of Independence—that all people are born equally free, with an overriding right to direct their own lives as they choose—Douglass became the primary advocate of the idea, articulated so well in King's "I Have A Dream" speech, that the solution for racial conflict in the United States is not separation, but for the nation to live out the true meaning of its founding creed. He had seen it happen before, when the shackles of slavery were riven and the Constitution amended to forever forbid that injustice. However pessimistic he may have felt when politicians elevated "practicality" over principle and ignored the reinstatement of slavery under lynch law, his faith in the fundamental rightness—and fundamental *possibility*—of those principles remained unshaken at the end. The Founding Fathers, he declared,

> were peace men; but they preferred revolution to peaceful submission to bondage. They were quiet men; but they did not shrink from agitating against oppression. They showed forbearance; but that they knew its limits. They believed in order; but not in the order of tyranny.

With them, nothing was "settled" that was not right. With them, justice, liberty and humanity were "final;" not slavery and oppression. You may well cherish the memory of such men. . . . They seized upon eternal principles, and set a glorious example in their defense. Mark them![31]

*Nothing is settled that is not right*. Time and tyranny have given us no reason to think otherwise.

# Notes

## Author's Note

[1]Waldo Martin, *The Mind of Frederick Douglass* (Chapel Hill: University of North Carolina Press, 1984), p. 67.

[2]James Oakes, "The Real Problem with White Abolitionists," *Jacobin*, Aug. 5, 2014, https://www.jacobinmag.com/2014/08/the-real-problem-with-white-abolitionists.

[3]Sacvan Bercovitch, *The Rites of Assent: Transformations in the Symbolic Construction of America* (New York: Routledge, 2013), p. 371. See also David W. Blight, *Frederick Douglass' Civil War: Keeping Faith in Jubilee* (Baton Rouge: University of Louisiana Press, 1989), pp. 232–33 (describing Douglass's individualism as a "contradiction" but concluding that Douglass "believed individualism could coexist with social justice").

[4]Frederick Douglass, "Self-Made Men" (Mar. 1893), in *The Frederick Douglass Papers: Series One: Speeches, Debates, and Interviews*, vol. 5, ed. J. W. Blassingame and John R. McKivigan IV (New Haven, CT: Yale University Press, 1991), p. 557.

## Introduction

[5]Henry Louis Gates, Jr., ed., *Douglass: Autobiographies* (New York: Library of America, 1994), p. 499.

[6]Ibid., p. 572.

[7]Ibid., p. 588.

[8]Frederick Douglass, "What the Black Man Wants" (Jan. 26, 1865), in *The Frederick Douglass Papers: Series One: Speeches, Debates, and Interviews*, vol. 4, ed. J. W. Blassingame and John R. McKivigan IV (New Haven, CT: Yale University Press, 1991), p. 69.

## Chapter 1

[1]Gates, ed., *Autobiographies*, p. 476.

[2]Ibid., p. 482.

[3]Ibid., p. 484.

[4]Mark Twain, *The Autobiography of Mark Twain*, vol. 1 (Berkeley: University of California Press, 2012), p. 32.

[5]William H. Freehling, *The Road to Disunion: Secessionists at Bay 1776–1854* (New York: Oxford University Press, 1990), p. 44.

[6]Frederick Douglass, "Lecture on Slavery" (Dec. 1, 1850), in *Frederick Douglass: Selected Speeches and Writings*, ed. Philip Foner and Yuval Taylor (Chicago: Lawrence Hill Books, 1999), p. 168.

[7]Dickson J. Preston, *Young Frederick Douglass* (Baltimore: Johns Hopkins University Press, 1980), ch. 4.

[8]Charles Edwards Lester, *Life and Public Services of Charles Sumner* (New York: United States Publishing Company, 1874), p. 479.

[9]Orlando Patterson, *Slavery and Social Death: A Comparative Study* (Cambridge, MA: Harvard University Press, 1985).

[10]Gates, ed., *Autobiographies*, p. 554.

[11]Ibid., p. 545.

[12]*State v. Mann*, 13 N.C. 263, 267 (1829).

[13]Gates, ed., *Autobiographies*, p. 295.

[14]Masters did, at times, pay slaves small amounts or allow them to keep items as theirs. But because these payments or claims could not be legally or even socially enforced, they were really revocable privileges, not property rights.

[15]David Waldstreicher, ed., *John Quincy Adams: Diaries*, vol. 1 (New York: Library of America, 2017), p. 544.

[16]Ibid.

[17]Kenneth Stampp, *The Peculiar Institution: Slavery in the Antebellum South* (New York: Vintage, 1956), p. 385.

[18]Gates, ed., *Autobiographies*, p. 496.

[19]Ibid., p. 514.

[20]Preston, *Young Frederick Douglass*, pp. 71–73.

[21]William McFeely, *Frederick Douglass* (New York: Norton, 1991), p. 24.

[22]Gates, ed., *Autobiographies*, p. 523.

[23]Ibid., p. 547.

[24]Ibid., p. 49.

[25]Robert S. Levine, *The Lives of Frederick Douglass* (Cambridge, MA: Harvard University Press, 2016), p. 282.

[26]William Wells Brown, *Narrative of William W. Brown, A Fugitive Slave* (1847), in *Slave Narratives*, ed. William L. Andrews and Henry Louis Gates, Jr. (New York: Library of America, 2000), p. 415.

[27]Quoted in Stephen Kendrick and Paul Kendrick, *Douglass and Lincoln: How a Revolutionary Black Leader and a Reluctant Liberator Struggled to End Slavery and Save the Union* (New York: Walker Books, 2008), p. 27.

[28]Gates, ed., *Autobiographies*, p. 346.

[29]Preston, *Young Frederick Douglass*, p. 65.

[30]Gates, ed., *Autobiographies*, p. 498.

[31]Ibid., p. 426.

## Chapter 2

[1]Gates, ed., *Autobiographies*, p. 216.

[2]Ibid., p. 527.

[3]Ibid. (emphasis added).

[4]Ibid., p. 530.

[5]Ibid., p. 44.

[6]Thomas Earl, ed., *The Life, Travels, and Opinions of Benjamin Lundy* (Philadelphia: William D. Parrish, 1847), pp. 207–8.

[7]Wendell Phillips Garrison and Francis Jackson Garrison, *William Lloyd Garrison: The Story of His Life*, vol. 1 (New York: Century, 1885), pp. 165–66.

[8]Louis P. Masur, *1831: Year of Eclipse* (New York: Hill & Wang, 2002).

[9]Gates, ed., *Autobiographies*, p. 537.

[10]Caleb Bingham, ed., *The Columbian Orator* (Baltimore: Philip H. Nicklin & Co., 1811), pp. 240–42.

[11]Gates, ed., *Autobiographies*, p. 535.

[12]Ibid., p. 554.

[13]Ibid., p. 557.

[14]Ibid., p. 99.

[15]Booker T. Washington, *Frederick Douglass* (1906; repr., Honolulu: University Press of the Pacific, 2003), p. 320.

[16]Frederic May Holland, *Frederick Douglass: The Colored Orator* (New York: Funk & Wagnolls, 1891), pp. 337–38.

[17]Gates, ed., *Autobiographies*, p. 560.

[18]Aleksandr Solzhenitsyn, *The Gulag Archipelago*, vol. 1, trans. Thomas P. Witney (New York: Harper & Row, 1974), pp. 103–17.

[19]Pierre Bourdieu, *Pascalian Meditations*, trans. Richard Nice (Stanford, CA: Stanford University Press, 2000), p. 228.

[20]Gates, ed., *Autobiographies*, pp. 59–60.

[21]Ibid., p. 58.

[22]Ibid., p. 574.

[23]Frederick Douglass, "Farewell Speech to the British People" (Mar. 30, 1847), in *Speeches and Writings*, p. 67.

[24]Gates, ed., *Autobiographies*, p. 598.

[25]Hannah Arendt, *The Origins of Totalitarianism* (Orlando, FL: Harcourt, rev. ed. 1976), p. 441.

[26]Gates, ed., *Autobiographies*, p. 580.

[27]Ibid., p. 578.

[28]Ibid.

[29]Ibid., p. 281.

[30]Ibid., p. 283.

[31]Ibid., p. 282.

[32]Ibid., p. 283.

[33]Ibid., p. 590.

[34]Ibid., p. 591.

[35]Ibid., p. 287.

## Chapter 3

[1]Gates, ed., *Autobiographies*, p. 598.

[2]Ibid., p. 307.

[3]Ibid.

[4]Ibid., p. 615.

[5]Ibid., p. 623.

[6]Preston, *Young Frederick Douglass*, pp. 146–47.

[7]Gates, ed., *Autobiographies*, p. 632.

[8]Ibid., p. 634.

[9]Ibid., p. 635.

[10]Ibid., p. 649.

[11]Booker T. Washington, *Up from Slavery* (New York: Doubleday, 1907), p. 23.

[12]Brown, *Narrative of a Fugitive Slave*, p. 417.

[13]Gates, ed., *Autobiographies*, p. 653.

[14]Alexis de Tocqueville, *Democracy in America*, trans. George Lawrence, ed. J. P. Mayer (New York: Harper & Row, 1969), p. 345.

[15]Ibid., p. 347.

[16]Ibid., p. 346.

[17]Ibid., p. 347.

[18]Ibid., p. 348.

[19]Douglass, "Self-Made Men," in *Frederick Douglass Papers*, vol. 5, p. 569.

[20]Ibid., p. 572.

[21]Gates, ed., *Autobiographies*, p. 358.

[22]Ibid., p. 654.

[23]Douglass, "What the Black Man Wants," in *Frederick Douglass Papers*, vol. 4, p. 61.

[24]Gates, ed., *Autobiographies*, p. 365.

[25]Douglass, "Self-Made Men," p. 550.

[26]Ibid.

## Chapter 4

[1]Henry Mayer, *All on Fire: William Lloyd Garrison and the Abolition of Slavery* (New York: St. Martin's Griffin, 1998).

[2]Thomas Jefferson, *Notes on the State of Virginia* (1787), in *Jefferson: Writings*, ed. Merrill Peterson (New York: Library of America, 1984), p. 264.

[3]Quoted in Blight, *Keeping Faith in Jubilee*, p. 127.

[4]William John Grayson, *The Hireling and the Slave, Chicora, and Other Poems* (Charleston, SC: McCarter & Co., 1856), pp. 22, 43–44.

[5]George Fitzhugh, *Sociology for the South: The Failure of a Free Society* (Richmond, VA: A. Morris, 1854), p. 7.

[6]Ibid., pp. 27–28.

[7]Ibid., p. 26.

[8]Mayer, *All on Fire*, p. 306.

[9]Gates, ed., *Autobiographies*, p. 367.

[10]Mayer (*All on Fire*, p. 374) remarks that while "it is tempting, but dangerous, to discern a racial dimension in the conflict and regard the abolitionist establishment as endeavoring to keep Douglass 'in his place,'" the Garrisonians' "anxiety" at Douglass's repudiation of their views "suggests that the radicals were afflicted not so much with racial bias as with the lingering effects of their sectarian warfare." Yet, Douglass was not alone in detecting racial bias in Garrison and his followers. Ibid., p. 433; John Stauffer, *The Black Hearts of Men* (Cambridge: Harvard University Press, 2004).

[11]Levine, *Lives of Frederick Douglass*, p. 61.

[12]Gates, ed., *Autobiographies*, p. 65.

[13]Frederick Douglass, "My Slave Experience in Maryland" (May 6, 1845), in *Speeches and Writings*, p. 14.

[14]Frederick Douglass, "Letter to William Lloyd Garrison" (Jan. 1, 1846), in *Speeches and Writings*, pp. 17–18.

[15]Gates, ed., *Autobiographies*, p. 668.

[16]Ibid., p. 673.

[17]Ibid.

[18]Lysander Spooner, *The Unconstitutionality of Slavery* (Boston: Bela Marsh, 1847); Gerrit Smith, *Letter of Gerrit Smith to Hon. Henry Clay* (New York: American Anti-Slavery Society, 1839); William Goodell, *Slavery and Anti-Slavery* (New York: William Harned, 1852); Joel Tiffany, *A Treatise on the Unconstitutionality of American Slavery* (Cleveland, OH: J. Calyer, 1849). Surprisingly little scholarship has been devoted to the anti-slavery constitutionalists. Among the best such scholars are William Wiecek, *The Sources of Antislavery Constitutionalism in America 1760–1848* (Ithaca, NY: Cornell University Press, 1977); Jacobus tenBroek, *Equal under Law* (New York: Collier, rev. ed. 1965); and Randy E. Barnett, "Was Slavery Unconstitutional before the Thirteenth Amendment? Lysander Spooner's Theory of Interpretation," *Pacific Law Journal* 28 (1997): 977–1014.

[19]Gates, ed., *Autobiographies*, p. 67.

[20]Ibid., p. 24.

[21]Ibid., p. 68.

## Chapter 5

[1]Richard Davis Webb, Letter to Maria Weston Chapman (May 16, 1846), Boston Public Library Rare Books Department, https://www.digital commonwealth.org/search/commonwealth:qz20vq71g.

[2]Gates, ed., *Autobiographies*, p. 375.

[3]Levine, *Lives of Frederick Douglass*, p. 106.

[4]Douglass, "Farewell Speech to the British People," in *Speeches and Writings*, pp. 57–58.

[5]Frederick Douglass, "The Right to Criticize American Institutions" (May 11, 1847), in *Speeches and Writings*, p. 78.

[6]Levine, *Lives of Frederick Douglass*, p. 110.

[7]Leigh Fought, *Women in the World of Frederick Douglass* (New York: Oxford University Press, 2017), pp. 86–87.

[8]Gates, ed., *Autobiographies*, p. 377.

[9]Julius E. Thompson et al., eds., *The Frederick Douglass Encyclopedia* (Santa Barbara, CA: Greenwood Press, 2010), p. 177.

[10]Frederick Douglass, "The *Dred Scott* Decision" (May 14, 1857), in *Speeches and Writings*, pp. 353–54.

[11]Timothy Sandefur, *The Conscience of the Constitution* (Washington: Cato Institute, 2014), pp. 46–47; Timothy Sandefur, "How Libertarians Should Think about the U.S. Civil War," *Reason Papers* 28 (2006): 61–83.

[12]See J. Cooke, ed., *The Federalist* (Middletown, CT: Wesleyan University Press, 1961), especially Nos. 15 and 33 (pp. 89–98, 203–8); Akhil Reed Amar, *America's Constitution: A Biography* (New York: Random House, 2005), pp. 5–53.

[13]*Dred Scott v. Sandford*, 60 U.S. 393 (1857).

[14]Gates, ed., *Autobiographies*, p. 762.

[15]Frederick Douglass, "Letter to Gerrit Smith" (Nov. 6, 1852), in *Speeches and Writings*, p. 210.

[16]Gates, *Autobiographies*, p. 717.

[17]Ibid, p. 719.

[18]Frederick Douglass, "The Anti-Slavery Movement" (Mar. 19, 1855), in *Speeches and Writings*, p. 327.

[19]Benjamin Quarles, *Frederick Douglass*, (1948; repr., New York: DaCapo, 1997), p. 105.

[20]Rosetta Douglass Sprague, "Anna Murray Douglass, My Mother as I Recall Her," Frederick Douglass Papers at the Library of Congress, p. 21, https://www.loc.gov/item/mfd.02007/.

[21]In 1856, a German émigré named Ottilie Assing arrived in New York to interview Douglass. She later moved to nearby Hoboken, and they continued their acquaintance for two and a half decades, enough to cause speculation ever since—some of it quite elaborate—about the nature of their connection. Assing herself seems to have fallen in love with Douglass. But he destroyed their letters, and what evidence exists suggests that theirs remained, if anything, an affair of the heart. Maria Diedrich's examination of his relationship with Ottilie Assing, *Love across the Color Lines* (New York: Hill & Wang, 1999), is almost entirely speculative—and substantially refuted by Leigh Fought's *Women in the World of Frederick Douglass*.

## Chapter 6

[1]Orlando Patterson, *Freedom in the Western World* (New York: Basic Books, 1992), p. 51.

[2]Ibid., p. 17.

[3]Frederick Douglass, "What to the Slave Is the Fourth of July?" in *Frederick Douglass Papers*, vol. 2, p. 385.

[4]*United States v. Fisher*, 6 U.S. 358, 390 (1805).

[5]Douglass, "What to the Slave Is the Fourth of July?," p. 386

[6]James Colaiaco, *Frederick Douglass and the Fourth of July* (New York: Palgrave Macmillan, 2006), p. 91.

[7] Quoted in James M. McPherson, *Battle Cry of Freedom* (Oxford, UK: Oxford University Press, 1988), p. 120.

[8] *Dred Scott v. Sandford*, 60 U.S. 393, 451–52 (1857).

[9] Frederick Douglass, "The *Dred Scott* Decision," p. 348.

[10] Ibid., p. 357.

[11] Ibid., p. 352.

[12] Ibid., p. 354.

[13] Ibid., p. 358.

[14] Frederick Douglass, "The Chicago Nominations," *Douglass' Monthly* (June 1860), in *Speeches and Writings*, pp. 392–93.

[15] Gates, ed., *Autobiographies*, p. 721.

[16] Douglass, "The Anti-Slavery Movement," in *Speeches and Writings*, pp. 324–25.

[17] John Stauffer et al., *Picturing Frederick Douglass: An Illustrated Biography of the Nineteenth Century's Most Photographed American* (New York: Liveright, 2015), p. 19.

[18] Quarles, *Frederick Douglass*, p. 180.

[19] Quoted in Kendrick and Kendrick, *Douglass and Lincoln*, p. 43.

[20] Fought, *Women in the World of Frederick Douglass*, pp. 172–73.

[21] Quoted in McFeely, *Frederick Douglass*, p. 207.

[22] Gates, ed., *Autobiographies*, p. 764.

[23] Douglass, "Chicago Nominations," in *Speeches and Writings*, p. 393.

[24] Douglass did prepare a speech in which he referred to Lincoln as the "black man's president," and he praised Lincoln for having recognized the rights of slaves over and above the effect slavery had on white America. But he never delivered the speech. See James Oakes, *The Radical and the Republican: Frederick Douglass, Abraham Lincoln, and the Triumph of Antislavery Politics* (New York: Norton, 2007), p. 256; Levine, *Lives of Frederick Douglass*, p. 239.

[25] Frederick Douglass, "The Fall of Sumter," *Douglass' Monthly* (May 1861), in *Speeches and Writings*, p. 444.

[26] Frederick Douglass, "The Future of the Negro People of the Slave States" (Feb. 5, 1862), in *Speeches and Writings*, p. 475.

[27] Frederick Douglass, "Letter to an English Correspondent" (June 1864), in *Speeches and Writings*, p. 568.

[28] Frederick Douglass, "Oration in Memory of Abraham Lincoln" (Apr. 14, 1876), in *Speeches and Writings*, p. 618.

[29] Frederick Douglass, "What Shall Be Done with the Slaves if Emancipated?" *Douglass' Monthly* (Jan. 1862), in *Speeches and Writings*, p. 471.

[30]Douglass, "Oration in Memory of Lincoln," pp. 621–22.

[31]Gates, ed., *Autobiographies*, p. 791.

[32]Douglass, "Oration in Memory of Abraham Lincoln," p. 620.

[33]Gates, ed., *Autobiographies*, p. 797.

[34]Frederick Douglass, "The Commander-in-Chief and His Black Soldiers," *Douglass' Monthly* (Aug. 1863), in *Speeches and Writings*, pp. 540–41.

[35]Gates, ed., *Autobiographies*, p. 817.

[36]Don E. Fehrenbacher, ed., *Lincoln: Speeches and Writings 1859–1865* (New York: Library of America, 1989), p. 624.

[37]Gates, ed., *Autobiographies*, p. 796.

[38]Ibid.

[39]Ibid., p. 804.

[40]David Herbert Donald, *Lincoln* (New York: Simon & Schuster, 1995), p. 576.

[41]Fehrenbacher, *Lincoln: Speeches and Writings*, p. 697.

[42]Ibid., p. 699.

[43]Frederick Douglass, "Hope and Despair in These Cowardly Times" (Apr. 28, 1861), in *Frederick Douglass Papers*, vol. 3, p. 425.

[44]Oakes, *The Radical and the Republican*, p. 245.

[45]Douglass, "Oration in Memory of Lincoln, in *Speeches and Writings*, p. 621.

[46]Fehrenbacher, *Lincoln: Speeches and Writings*, p. 687.

## Chapter 7

[1]Frederick Douglass, "The Mission of the War" (Jan. 14, 1864), in *Speeches and Writings*, p. 565.

[2]Gates, ed., *Autobiographies*, p. 802.

[3]Douglas R. Egerton, *The Wars of Reconstruction* (New York: Bloomsbury Press, 2014), p. 18.

[4]Frederick Douglass, "The Need for Continuing Anti-Slavery Work" (May 10, 1865), in *Speeches and Writings*, pp. 578–79.

[5]Ibid., p. 103.

[6]Egerton, *The Wars of Reconstruction*, p. 194.

[7]Frederick Douglass, "Reply of the Colored Delegation to the President" (Feb. 7, 1866), in *Speeches and Writings*, p. 589.

[8]Blight, *Keeping Faith in Jubilee*, pp. 201–2.

[9]Martin, *Mind of Frederick Douglass*, p. 67.

[10]That was ultimately what happened a century later, when racially restrictive zoning laws, and then federal and state "urban renewal"

projects, sought to sequester and then evict black landowners to eradicate "urban blight." See Justice Clarence Thomas's dissenting opinion in *Kelo v. New London*, 545 U.S. 469, 505 (2005).

[11]Gates, ed., *Autobiographies*, p. 634.

[12]Frederick Douglass, "Coming Home" (June 17, 1877), in *Frederick Douglass Papers*, vol. 4, p. 480.

[13]Frederick Douglass, "Property in Soil and Property in Man" (Nov. 18, 1848), in *The Life and Writings of Frederick Douglass*, vol. 5, ed. Philip S. Foner (New York: International Publishers, 1975), pp. 105–6.

[14]Holland, *Frederick Douglass*, pp. 91–92. While these are Holland's words, Douglass lauded the book as doing him "scrupulous justice." Gates, ed., *Autobiographies*, p. 943.

[15]Frederick Douglass, "A Reform Absolutely Complete," Apr. 9, 1870, *Frederick Douglass Papers*, vol. 4, p. 265.

[16]Douglass, "What the Black Man Wants," in *Frederick Douglass Papers*, vol. 4, pp. 68–69.

[17]Blight, *Keeping Faith in Jubilee*, p. 202.

[18]*Speeches and Writings*, p. 261.

[19]Douglass, "Self-Made Men," p. 557.

[20]Quoted in Fought, *Women in the World of Frederick Douglass* p. 136.

[21]Douglass, "Seeming and Real," Oct. 6, 1870, in *Speeches and Writings*, p. 607.

[22]For example, although he long opposed proposals to outlaw alcohol, on the grounds that "enforced morality is artificial morality," toward the end of his life, he changed his mind and endorsed prohibition. Holland, *Frederick Douglass*, p. 400; Nicholas Buccola, *The Political Thought of Frederick Douglass* (New York: NYU Press, 2012), p. 50.

[23]Eric Foner, *Free Soil, Free Labor, Free Men: The Ideology of the Republican Party before the Civil War* (Oxford, UK: Oxford University Press, 1995).

[24]Buccola, *Political Thought*, p. 119, (citing Deirdre McCloskey, *The Bourgeois Virtues: Ethics for an Age of Commerce* (Chicago: University of Chicago Press, 2007).

[25]Quoted in McFeely, *Frederick Douglass*, p. 246.

[26]Thomas G. West, *Vindicating the Founders* (Lanham, MD: Rowman & Littlefield, 2001), pp. 74–77.

[27]Ellen Carol DuBois and Richard Candida, eds., *Elizabeth Cady Stanton, Feminist as Thinker: A Reader in Documents and Essays* (New York: NYU Press, 2007), p. 197.

[28]Philip S. Foner, ed., "Proceedings of the American Equal Rights Association Convention, May 12, 1869," in *Frederick Douglass on Women's Rights* (New York: Da Capo, 1992), p. 87.

[29]Quarles, *Frederick Douglass*, p. 251.

[30]Charles Sumner, "Letter to Gerrit Smith" (July 9, 1872), in Octavius Brooks Frothingham, *Gerrit Smith: A Biography*, 3rd ed. (New York: G. P. Putnam's Sons, 1877), pp. 322–23.

[31]Quarles (*Frederick Douglass*, p. 260) erroneously reports the opposite.

[32]Frederick Douglass, "There Was a Right Side in the Late War" (May 30, 1878), in *Speeches and Writings*, p. 629.

[33]Gates, ed., *Autobiographies*, p. 963.

[34]Frederick Douglass, "Give Us the Freedom Intended for Us" (Dec. 5, 1872), in *Speeches and Writings*, p. 613.

## Chapter 8

[1]Blight, *Keeping Faith in Jubilee*, p. 199.

[2]Douglass, "Self-Made Men," in *Frederick Douglass Papers*, vol. 5, p. 565.

[3]Frederick Douglass, "The Nation's Problem" (Apr. 16, 1889), in *Speeches and Writings*, p. 730.

[4]Ta-Nehisi Coates, "Frederick Douglass: American Lion," *Atlantic*, September 26, 2011, https://www.theatlantic.com/national/archive/2011/09/frederick-douglass-american-lion/245653/. Coates does regard Douglass as among "the tradition of radical progressives." Ibid. The term "progressive," however, is misleading when used—as, for instance, Douglas Egerton repeatedly does—to describe nineteenth-century classical liberals such as Douglass or Sumner. The term usually refers to such twentieth-century advocates of government regulation and social reform as Woodrow Wilson or Theodore Roosevelt, who were not just hostile to the views of Reconstruction-era Republicans, but—at least in Wilson's case—were advocates of segregation and racial subordination. In fact, twentieth-century progressives established segregation as we know it. See Michael McGerr, *A Fierce Discontent: The Rise and Fall of the Progressive Movement in America* (New York: Free Press, 2003), ch. 6.

[5]Peter F. Walker, *Moral Choices: Memory, Desire, and Imagination in Nineteenth Century American Abolition* (Baton Rouge: Louisiana State University Press, 1978), p. 247. See also Houston A. Baker, *The Journey Back: Issues in Black Literature and Criticism* (Chicago: University of Chicago Press, 1980), pp. 36–43. Baker argues that Douglass's use of language was "conditioned by white, Christian standards" so that it obscured his real self: "for

once literacy has been achieved, the black self is "transformed." "Had there been a separate black written language available," Baker concludes, "Douglass might have fared better." Of course, had there been one, Douglass would have refused to use it. He would likely have said that the black self was *freed*, not confined, by literacy.

[6]Martin, *Mind of Frederick Douglass*, p. 134.

[7]Gates, ed., *Autobiographies*, p. 954.

[8]Douglass, "The Nation's Problem," in *Speeches and Writings*, p. 731.

[9]Ta-Nehisi Coates, "The First White President," *Atlantic*, October 2017, p. 74.

[10]Frederick Douglass, "The Lessons of the Hour," in *Frederick Douglass Papers*, vol. 5, pp. 600–601.

[11]Frederick Douglass, "Why Is the Negro Lynched?" *The Lesson of the Hour* (1894), in *Speeches and Writings*, p. 760.

[12]Buccola, *Political Thought*, p. 11.

[13]Frederick Douglass, "The Country Has Not Heard the Last of P. B. S. Pinchback," in *Frederick Douglass Papers*, vol. 4, p. 424.

[14]Gates, ed., *Autobiographies*, p. 860.

[15]Booker T. Washington, *Frederick Douglass* (Philadelphia: George W. Jacobs & Co., 1906), p. 290.

[16]Levine, *Lives of Frederick Douglass*, chap. 5.

[17]Douglass, "There Was a Right Side in the Late War," in *Speeches and Writings*, p. 631.

[18]Ibid., p. 632.

[19]Gates, ed., *Autobiographies*, p. 948.

[20]Ibid., p. 963.

[21]Douglass, "The United States Cannot Remain Half-Slave and Half-Free" (Apr. 16, 1883), in *Speeches and Writings*, p. 657.

[22]Gates, ed., *Autobiographies*, p. 864.

[23]Frederick Douglass, "Address to the People of the United States" (Sep. 25, 1883), in *Speeches and Writings*, p. 673.

[24]Ibid., p. 675.

[25]Ibid.

[26]Ibid., pp. 681–82.

[27]109 U.S. 3 (1883).

[28]Frederick Douglass, "The Civil Rights Case" (Oct. 22, 1883), in *Speeches and Writings*, pp. 689–91.

[29]John Edward Bruce, in *The Washington Grit*, Feb. 16, 1884.

[30]Gates, ed., *Autobiographies*, p. 961.

[31]Afreda M. Duster, ed., *Crusade for Justice: The Autobiography of Ida B. Wells* (Chicago: University of Chicago Press, 1970), pp. 72–73.

[32]Gates, ed., *Autobiographies*, p. 962.

## Chapter 9

[1]Gates, ed., *Autobiographies*, p. 959.

[2]Ibid., p. 1012.

[3]Ibid., p. 1014.

[4]Ibid., p. 1021.

[5]Ibid., p. 1020.

[6]Ibid., p. 1045.

[7]David Brion Davis, *Inhuman Bondage: The Rise and Fall of Slavery in the New World* (New York: Oxford University Press, 2006), p. 174.

[8]David Walker, *Walker's Appeal*, 3rd ed. (Boston: David Walker, 1830), p. 24.

[9]Gates, ed., *Autobiographies*, p. 1031.

[10]Ibid., p. 1034.

[11]Ibid., p. 1033.

[12]Robert Rydell, *All the World's a Fair: Visions of Empire at American International Expositions, 1876–1916* (Chicago: University of Chicago Press, 1984), pp. 59–60.

[13]"Appeal of Douglass," *Chicago Tribune*, Aug. 26, 1893, p. 3.

[14]Newspapers reported at the time that Dunbar read a poem called "Colored Americans," but there is no such poem. His biographer, Virginia Cunningham, believes he read "The Colored Soldiers." Virginia Cunningham, *Paul Laurence Dunbar and His Song* (New York: Dodd, Mead & Co. 1947), p. 104.

[15]Quoted in Robert W. Rydell, ed., *The Reason Why the Colored American Is Not in the World's Columbian Exposition* (Urbana: University of Illinois Press, 1999), p. xxii.

[16]Duster, *Crusade for Justice*, p. 72.

[17]Ibid., p. 119.

[18]Booker T. Washington, *My Larger Education* (Garden City, NY: Doubleday, 1911), pp. 57–58.

[19]Washington, *Up from Slavery*, pp. 221–22.

[20]W. E. B. DuBois, *The Souls of Black Folk*, 8th ed. (Chicago: A. C. McClurg, Co., 1909), pp. 49–50.

[21]Quoted in Robert J. Norrell, *Up from History: The Life of Booker T. Washington* (Cambridge, MA: Belknap, 2009), p. 6.

[22]Kelly Miller, *Race Adjustment: Essays on the Negro in America* (New York: Neale, 1908), p. 18.

[23]Norrell, *Up from History*, p. 439.

[24]Washington, *Up from Slavery*, p. 224.

[25]Norrell, *Up from History*, p. 167.

[26]Washington, *Up from Slavery*, p. 236.

[27]Douglass, "The Nation's Problem," in *Speeches and Writings*, p. 731.

[28]Ibid., pp. 729–31.

[29]Douglass, "Lessons of the Hour," in *Frederick Douglass Papers*, vol. 5, p. 577.

[30]Ibid., p. 590.

[31]Ibid., p. 578.

[32]Ibid., p. 595.

[33]Ibid., p. 596.

[34]Ibid.

[35]Ibid., p. 598.

[36]Ibid., p. 607.

[37]John Aaron Wright, *Discovering African American St. Louis: A Guide to Historic Sites* (St. Louis: Missouri History Museum, 2002), p. 148; "Swung Him Up," *St. Louis Post-Dispatch*, Jan. 17, 1894, p. 1.

## Chapter 10

[1]Buccola, *Political Thought*, p. 101. The story does have basis in fact. In 1852, Douglass told an Ohio audience that the most important anti-slavery work was "agitation. Agitate, *agitate*. This is the grand instrumentality, and without this you Free Soilers will come to nothing." Frederick Douglass, "Agitate, Agitate" (Aug. 23, 1852), in *Frederick Douglass Papers*, vol. 2, p. 396.

[2]Douglass took little notice of this. He disapproved of Woodhull and supported Grant for the presidency. Fought, *Women in the World of Frederick Douglass*, p. 202.

[3]Frederick Douglass, "I am a Radical Woman Suffrage Man" (May 28, 1888), in *The Frederick Douglass Papers: Series One: Speeches, Debates, and Interviews*, vol. 5, ed. J. W. Blassingame and John R. McKivigan IV (New Haven, CT: Yale University Press, 1991), p. 383

[4]*Buchanan v. Warley*, 245 U.S. 60 (1917). See Damon Root, *Overruled* (New York: Palgrave MacMillan, 2014), pp. 57–61.

[5]Edmund Morris, *Theodore Rex* (New York: Random House, 2001), p. 55.

[6]Gary W. Gallegher and Alan T. Nolan, eds., *The Myth of the Lost Cause and Civil War History* (Bloomington: Indiana University Press, 2010); John McKee Barr, *Loathing Lincoln* (Baton Rouge: Louisiana State University Press, 2014), pp. 59–61, 115–17.

[7]Jefferson Davis, *The Rise and Fall of the Confederate Government*, vol. 1 (New York: Appleton & Co., 1881), p. 78.

[8]Ibid.

[9]Mississippi Ordinance of Secession, in *Proceedings of the Mississippi State Convention* (Jackson: Power & Cadwallader, 1861), p. 4.

[10]Alexander Stephens, "Corner Stone Speech" (Mar. 21, 1861) (Ashland, OH: Ashbrook Center), http://teachingamericanhistory.org/library /document/cornerstone-speech/.

[11]Eric Foner, *Reconstruction: America's Unfinished Revolution, 1863–1877* (New York: Harper & Row, 1988), p. 610.

[12]Charles Edward Merriam, *History of American Political Theories* (New York: Macmillan, 1903), p. 250.

[13]Woodrow Wilson, "Edmund Burke: The Man and His Times," in *Woodrow Wilson: Essential Writings and Speeches of the Scholar President*, ed. Mario R. DiNunzio (New York: NYU Press, 2006), p. 90.

[14]Woodrow Wilson, "States Rights," in *Essential Writings and Speeches of the Scholar President*, p. 201.

[15]Woodrow Wilson, "John Bright," in *Essential Writings and Speeches of the Scholar President*, p. 73.

[16]Ibid., p. 207.

[17]Woodrow Wilson, "The Reconstruction of the Southern States," in *Essential Writings and Speeches of the Scholar President*, pp. 206–7.

[18]Gary Gerstle, "Race and Nation in the Thought and Politics of Woodrow Wilson," in *Reconsidering Woodrow Wilson: Progressivism, Internationalism, War, and Peace*, ed. John M. Cooper Jr. (Washington: Woodrow Wilson International Center for Scholars, 2008), p. 121.

[19]Dick Lehr, "The Racist Legacy of Woodrow Wilson," *Atlantic*, Nov. 27, 2015.

[20]With the exception of a single scene in the 1989 film *Glory*, he has never even been portrayed in a major motion picture. He was also portrayed in some scenes of the 2017 Series *Underground*.

[21]Blight, *Keeping Faith in Jubilee*, p. 117 n. 28.

[22]Keith D. Miller, *Voice of Deliverance: The Language of Martin Luther King, Jr., and Its Sources* (Athens: University of Georgia Press, 1998), pp. 199–200.

[23]Martin Luther King, Jr., "The Negro and the Constitution" (May 1944), in *The Papers of Martin Luther King, Jr.*, vol. 1, ed. Clayborne Carson et al. (Berkeley: University of California Press, 1992), p. 111.

[24]Peter C. Myers, *Frederick Douglass: Race and the Rebirth of American Liberalism* (Lawrence: University Press of Kansas, 2008), p. 7.

[25]Frederick Douglass, "What to the Slave Is the Fourth of July?" p. 364.

[26]Martin, *Mind of Frederick Douglass*, p. 282.

[27]Charles W. Mills, "Whose Fourth of July? Frederick Douglass and 'Original Intent,'" in *Frederick Douglass: A Critical Reader*, ed. Bill E. Lawson and Frank M. Kirkland (Malden, MA: Blackwell, 1999), pp. 102, 115, 121.

[28]Myers, *Race and the Rebirth of American Liberalism*, p. 196.

[29]Ibid., p. 292.

[30]Douglass, "Self-Made Men," in *Frederick Douglass Papers*, vol. 5, p. 571.

[31]Douglass, "What to the Slave Is the Fourth of July?" pp. 364–65.

# Index

Note: Information in endnotes is indicated by n.

# About the Author

Timothy Sandefur is Vice President for Litigation at the Goldwater Institute's Scharf-Norton Center for Constitutional Litigation, where he also holds the Duncan Chair in Constitutional Government. He is the author of *Cornerstone of Liberty: Property Rights in 21st Century America* (coauthored with Christina Sandefur, 2016), *The Right to Earn A Living* (2010), *The Conscience of The Constitution* (2014), and *The Permission Society* (2016), and dozens of scholarly articles on subjects ranging from eminent domain and economic liberty to antitrust, copyright, and the political philosophy in Shakespeare, ancient Greek drama, and *Star Trek*.

# Cato Institute

Founded in 1977, the Cato Institute is a public policy research foundation dedicated to broadening the parameters of policy debate to allow consideration of more options that are consistent with the principles of limited government, individual liberty, and peace. To that end, the Institute strives to achieve greater involvement of the intelligent, concerned lay public in questions of policy and the proper role of government.

The Institute is named for *Cato's Letters*, libertarian pamphlets that were widely read in the American Colonies in the early 18th century and played a major role in laying the philosophical foundation for the American Revolution.

Despite the achievement of the nation's Founders, today virtually no aspect of life is free from government encroachment. A pervasive intolerance for individual rights is shown by government's arbitrary intrusions into private economic transactions and its disregard for civil liberties. And while freedom around the globe has notably increased in the past several decades, many countries have moved in the opposite direction, and most governments still do not respect or safeguard the wide range of civil and economic liberties.

To address those issues, the Cato Institute undertakes an extensive publications program on the complete spectrum of policy issues. Books, monographs, and shorter studies are commissioned to examine the federal budget, Social Security, regulation, military spending, international trade, and myriad other issues. Major policy conferences are held throughout the year, from which papers are published thrice yearly in the *Cato Journal*. The Institute also publishes the quarterly magazine *Regulation*.

In order to maintain its independence, the Cato Institute accepts no government funding. Contributions are received from foundations, corporations, and individuals, and other revenue is generated from the sale of publications. The Institute is a nonprofit, tax-exempt, educational foundation under Section 501(c)3 of the Internal Revenue Code.

CATO INSTITUTE
1000 Massachusetts Ave., N.W.
Washington, D.C. 20001
www.cato.org